TH SHORTEST HISTORY OF GREECE

The Odyssey of a Nation from Myth to Modernity

JAMES HENEAGE

THE EXPERIMENT

NEW YORK

To Georgia

The Experiment, LLC
220 East 23rd Street, Suite 600
New York, NY 10010-4658
theexperimentpublishing.com

Library of Congress Cataloging-in-Publication Data

Names: Heneage, James, author.
Title: The shortest history of Greece : the odyssey of a nation from myth
  to modernity / James Heneage.
Description: New York : The Experiment, 2023. | Series: The shortest
  history series | Originally published: Great Britain : Old Street
  Publishing Ltd, 2022. First published in North America in revised form
  by The Experiment, LLC, 2023. | Includes bibliographical references and
  index.
Identifiers: LCCN 2022050106 (print) | LCCN 2022050107 (ebook) | ISBN
  9781615199488 (paperback) | ISBN 9781615199495 (ebook)
Subjects: LCSH: Greece--History.
Classification: LCC DF757 .H46 2023 (print) | LCC DF757 (ebook) | DDC
  949.5--dc23/eng/20221018
LC record available at https://lccn.loc.gov/2022050106
LC ebook record available at https://lccn.loc.gov/2022050107

ISBN 978-1-61519-948-8
Ebook ISBN 978-1-61519-949-5

Cover and text design by Jack Dunnington

Manufactured in the United States of America

First printing March 2023
10 9 8 7 6 5 4 3 2 1

Contents

Preface

> When, on his way to Thebes, Oedipus encountered the Sphinx, his answer to its riddle was: Man. That simple word destroyed the monster. We have many monsters to destroy. Let us think of the answer of Oedipus.
>
> George Seferis, Nobel Prize acceptance speech, 1963

Long before history, Zeus sent a pair of eagles to fly around the world. Wherever they met would be its center, and there an oracle would sit to pronounce on the affairs of men. Delphi was that place, not far to the west of Athens, and for a thousand years its oracle did just that.

The oracle's main message was "Know thyself." For Aristotle, that meant knowing that man was a "social animal" who without community became either "beast or god." This insight underpinned a new idea about how men should govern themselves: *demokratia*. It was a good idea, so good that a vital part of it endured even after a devastating civil war had opened the door for tyranny to return. *Demokratia*, it seemed, brought not only purpose to lives, but also beauty and meaning. It empowered men (only men at that time) not just to govern themselves but to create great art and science too.

Wherever Greeks went, the idea of human empowerment went with them, and they traveled far and wide. So Alexander the Great's empire became Greek, just as the Roman Empire became the Greek one that saved Europe from conquest. The Renaissance courts of Northern Italy drew inspiration from the Greeks, as did the *philosophes* of the European Enlightenment.

The West owes its civilization to the Greeks. It's a debt we often tell ourselves we have repaid: by supporting Greece's struggle for independence and the nation's expansion in the nineteenth century; her stand against Nazi tyranny, postwar boom, and joining of the European Union in the twentieth. But this support has seldom been disinterested, and it has sometimes come at great cost to the Greek people. After the Second World War, Britain and America helped bring about a civil war whose legacy was half a century of political turmoil and the worst financial crisis ever endured by an advanced economy. The harsh terms that were attached to Greece's "rescue" from that crisis suggest that Europe now considers its debt fully settled.

It isn't. Over the coming decades, our democracy will be tested as never before. In its current guise it is unlikely to survive. I have written this book because I believe that the story of the Greeks—ancient, modern, and contemporary—can help us reinvent it.

PART ONE

Ruling Half the World

BEGINNINGS–1453

THE HOMERIC AGE

> These things never happened, but always are.
>
> Sallust, Roman philosopher, 4th century CE

It is 1000 BCE and you are sitting beneath a wall made of stones only giants could have lifted. Thunder and lightning rend the night and a bitter wind scatters sparks from the fire that warms you. You shiver and wonder. Who built this wall I sit beneath? What makes the thunder? How did I learn to make this fire? To whom or what do I owe the beauty and misery of my existence? Someone sits down beside you. He is the traveling bard, and he has the answers. Through the night he will recite them in poetry that you know almost by heart.

He'll talk of *Chaos* that came before everything, then the first incestuous coupling that brought forth the world. How *Gaia* (Earth) and her son *Uranus* (Sky), gave birth to twelve Titans—six males and six females—plus a race of one-eyed Cyclopes and some giants, each with a hundred hands. It was they who built the wall with its huge stones.

The work of giants: Cyclopean stones at Mycenae

One of the Titans, Cronus, rebelled against his father and castrated him, then married his own sister, Rhea, by whom he had the first generation of Greek gods. But Cronus kept eating his offspring, fearing a repeat of what he'd done to his father. So Rhea spirited away her newborn Zeus, giving her husband a wrapped stone to swallow instead. Zeus came back with a potion that made Cronus vomit up the stone along with all his siblings. He banished his father and, true to tradition, took his sister Hera for wife.

Eventually, after battling it out with the Titans, Zeus and Hera came to rule over ten senior gods on Mount Olympus. There they consumed nectar and ambrosia and interfered in the affairs of mankind, not always to its benefit. It was Prometheus, a Titan, not a god, who gave us fire. Zeus was so angry that he chained him to a rock, his liver to be daily pecked out by an eagle.

Next was a time of mortal heroes. Most were men and most had a god for parent. Perseus, Oedipus, Jason, and Theseus battled with giants, sphinxes, gorgons, and dragons to make the world safe for humans. Prometheus was eventually set free from his chains by the greatest hero of them all: Heracles.

Gorgon's head: architectural ornament from Thassos, c. 4th century BCE

The Greeks looked to their gods to explain their world, to answer the questions posed by thunder and lightning, earthquake and drought. It was to them they gave thanks for the change of seasons and the glory of the heavens at night. The Milky Way (*Galaxias*), for example, was splashed across the nocturnal sky when Hera pulled the enormous baby Heracles from her teat. They looked to the gods, too, for answers to the questions posed by being mortal: the emotions, motives, and contradictions that make us who we are. It helped that these gods were as imperfect as those they ruled over. They too loved, schemed, lusted, envied, and took their revenge. Their moral instruction was limited and practical. Give hospitality (*xenia*) to the stranger who knocks at your door, they said, since he might just be Zeus in disguise.

The great German scholar of Greek mythology, Walter Burkert, described myth as a "traditional tale with a secondary, practical reference to something of collective importance." The gods helped the Greeks to understand not just their world, but themselves. "Know thyself," prescribed the Oracle. It was the first step toward self-government.

From Myth to History

The Greek Bronze Age (3000–1000 BCE) saw three extraordinary civilizations: Cycladic, Minoan, and Mycenaean. It was the Minoan that gave Europe her founding myth. It told of a Phoenician princess, Europa, who was gathering flowers when the ever-randy Zeus, on this occasion disguised as a beautiful white bull, carried her off to Greece to seduce her. She became the first queen of Crete and mother of King Minos, from whom the words Minoan and Minotaur are derived. Zeus so loved her that he painted himself among the stars in the shape of a bull—Taurus.

Cycladic culture 3000–1900 BCE
Minoan culture 2500–1400 BCE
Mycenaean culture 1700–1100 BCE

Troy

Mycenae

Akrotiri

Crete

Knossos

The historical Minoan civilization of Crete (2500–1400 BCE) seems to have been a peaceful trading culture. Figurines show a caste of powerful, snake-wielding female priests, who are generally larger than their darker-skinned male counterparts. Exquisite frescoes from the Minoan settlement of Akrotiri on Santorini suggest a sea-faring civilization given to fishing, celebration, and commerce.

The Akrotiri Monkeys

How far afield did the Minoans trade? The picture is still changing. Frescoes found at Akrotiri depict monkeys with S-shaped tails that look very similar to the grey langurs of the Indus Valley. At the time when the Minoans were exporting luxury goods, such as the purple dye made from Murex sea snails farmed off Crete, the rich Bronze Age Harappan civilization was thriving on the banks of the Indus. Is it possible that some Minoan merchant took a cargo of snails to the East, and came back with monkeys?

Minoan monkey tails: wall fresco from Akrotiri, c. 17th century BCE

The Mycenaean civilization was very different. It began around 1700 BCE when the Achaeans, an eastern steppe people, migrated south and settled in the Peloponnese, the claw attached to the bottom of Greece by a skinny wrist of land they named the *isthmos*. Their society was hierarchical, with a warrior elite devoted to horses, and they built fortified settlements, the most famous of which were at Mycenae and Tiryns. The giant stones they used gave the name Cyclopean to this style of architecture, since later Greeks imagined only giants could have lifted them. At some point, the Mycenaeans took to the sea and came into contact with the Minoans, who introduced them to the advantages of trade.

Around 1600 BCE, the Minoan civilization was fatally damaged by a huge eruption on the island of Thera (today's Santorini), which buried Akrotiri's monkeys under ash. The Mycenaean Empire, though, continued to flourish, reaching its apogee in the twelfth century BCE, by which time it had spawned settlements across the Aegean, right up to the shores of Asia Minor. "Like ants or frogs around a pond," Plato would write almost a millennium later.

The Shipwreck and the Script

In the summer of 1982, a young sponge diver from the village of Yalikavak, near Bodrum in Turkey, chanced upon one of history's most spectacular shipwrecks. Mehmed Çakır discovered the remains of a 14th-century BCE vessel that had probably sunk on its way from a port in the Levant to a Mycenaean palace in Greece. It was carrying a cargo of luxury items ranging from African hippopotamus teeth to jewelry from Canaan. The Greek Peloponnese was at the heart of a trading network that connected the great civilizations of Egypt and Mesopotamia—and possibly India, if the tails of the Akrotiri monkeys do not deceive.

Also found in the shipwreck was a small boxwood writing tablet engraved with the mysterious Linear B script. Its deciphering in 1952 is attributed to the British architect Michael Ventris, but much of the legwork was done by Alice Kober, an academic from New York. In the 1930s, Kober began work on samples that had been found fire-baked into tablets in palaces throughout the Peloponnese. Having mastered Hittite, Akkadian, Old Irish, Tocharian, Sumerian, Old Persian, Basque, and Chinese, she assembled a database in forty notebooks on 180,000 cards, using cigarette cards when paper was rationed during the war.* After her death, her work was used by Ventris, who, with the addition of some inspired guesswork, deciphered the script in 1952 and established it as Mycenaean Greek.

The signs and ideograms of Linear B were used mainly to record the distribution of goods such as wool and grain to customers. They bear witness to a talent for organized trade that perhaps reached as far as India.

---

* Perhaps it is no surprise to learn that Kober was a chain smoker. She died in 1950 at the age of 43.

This Linear B tablet was baked, and thus preserved, by the fire that destroyed the Palace of Pylos, c. 1200 BCE.

Iliad and Odyssey

Homer's epics are vital staging posts on the Greek journey from myth into history. The two poems are set toward the end of the Greek Bronze Age, when the Mycenaeans might well have crossed paths with the mighty Hittite Empire, of which the city of Troy (*Ilios*) may have been a western outpost. On the Aegean coast of modern Turkey, just over a hundred miles from today's Greek border, it would have made an attractive target for pillage.

The *Iliad* describes a few crucial weeks toward the end of the ten-year siege of Troy, when the Greeks are on the point of losing the war. Everything turns on whether the semi-divine Achilles—their one-man blitzkrieg—can be persuaded to abandon literature's longest sulk to rejoin the fight. The target of his anger is King Agamemnon, who has dishonored him by exercising *droit du seigneur* over his concubine Briseis, the spoil of a previous battle.

When Achilles finally leaves his tent, it isn't because Agamemnon has apologized, but to avenge the death of his best friend, Patroclus, who has been killed by the Trojan champion, Hector. The gods intervene decisively in the encounter, as they do throughout the tale, but their interventions are capricious and unpredictable, following the twists and turns of their own internecine squabbles on Mount Olympus. They are like super-powers using the clashes of smaller nations to fight a proxy war. Achilles wades through oceans of blood to exact his revenge, mutilating and dishonoring Hector's corpse in a frenzy of grief and rage. Soon afterward, though, he is visited in his tent by Hector's grieving father, King Priam of Troy, who begs for the return of his son's body. Against all expectations, Achilles is moved by pity and gives Hector back.

The *Odyssey* is very different. More human and intimate, it tells of Odysseus's perilous journey home from Troy to the small island of Ithaca. He survives sea monsters, whirlpools, witches, and cannibals—and the wrath of the sea god, Poseidon—only to find himself in the midst of another siege, that of his wife Penelope by 108 rowdy suitors. Odysseus defeats (and kills) them all in an archery contest, winning back both wife and kingdom.

What makes these two stories so important? Millions of words have been written on this subject, but perhaps it comes down what they have to say about a single question. Who decides our fate—the gods, or us?

The first word of the *Iliad* in Greek is "wrath" (*minin*) and many of the next sixteen thousand lines seem to be part of a vast hymn to rage. Yet the whole story hinges on the moment when rage dissolves into grief and pity, as Achilles allows Priam to remove his son's body and give him a proper burial. This is the moment when Achilles puts divinity behind him and embraces the business of being human, which is the business of grief and pity. At the start of the poem, he is more god than human, son of the sea goddess Thetis. By the end, he is the very mortal son of his mortal father, Peleus, and able to feel another father's grief. The age of gods is over, and the age of man can begin.

In the *Odyssey*, composed later, humans are firmly at center stage. Events are driven by the dangerous adventures that thwart the hero's longed-for homecoming. It reflects a time when the Greeks were founding new homes across the known world, when it felt vital to define what it meant to be Greek.

Whether the two poems were authored by a man called Homer or emerged from a collective folk tradition, their form was more or less fixed in the sixth century BCE. They were recited again and again at festivals and other public events, including over consecutive nights at the Olympic games. Together they speak of the Greeks' first steps toward taking responsibility for their world. They underpin later Greek political thinking, playing a vital part in the growth of a system that put citizen participation at its very core.

Milman Parry (1902–35)

It was another eccentric American academic who established that Homer must have been working in an oral tradition. Milman Parry toured the Balkans on great recording adventures, listening to traditional poetry sung to the one-stringed *gusle* (and later reciting it under the stars to his long-suffering family). He revealed the oral poet's tricks of the trade. Stock phrases such as *eos rhododaktylos* (rosy-fingered dawn) or *podas okus achilleus* (swift-footed Achilles) served to keep the bard within the metrical pattern and helped his extempore composition.

Parry's painstaking work also contributed to our understanding of the *Iliad* as something older than the *Odyssey*—a story reaching back to a time when the Greeks' ancestors were migrating west across the steppes, and when the horse, not the sea, was the dominant feature of their lives.

Collapse

The Mycenaean civilization collapsed around 1100 BCE, to be followed by three centuries often called the Greek Dark Age. The cause of the breakdown could have been civil war or climate change, or a combination. Or perhaps it was the result of some attritional war, of which Troy became the mythic record. The most attractive hypothesis involves the mysterious "sea peoples," yet to be firmly identified, who laid waste to much of the eastern Mediterranean around that time and may have burned down the palaces in which the baked Linear B tablets were found.

THE ARCHAIC AGE (776–500 BCE)

Growth of the Polis

Into the darkness rushed the Dorians, from around 1100 BCE. Where the tribe came from is anyone's guess, though Herodotus tells us it was Macedonia. They poured into the Peloponnese, bypassing the Ionians, who'd chosen Attica for their home.

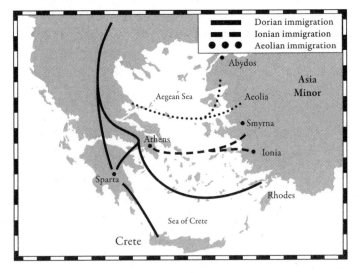

As the Mycenaeans were to the Minoans, the Dorians were to the Ionians. The former were militaristic arrivistes, the latter a settled trading people. Only an isthmus separated them, and though the two would never merge, their temporary partnership would bring forth the miracle of the Greek Classical Age.

From about 800 BCE, both began building cities (*poleis*), often upon Mycenaean ruins. The Dorians built Sparta, while the Ionians chose a rock named after Athena, goddess of wisdom. Legend has it that Poseidon, brother of Zeus, also wanted patronage of the city, so the two deities went head-to-head, competing to see who could offer the Athenians the best future. Poseidon drove his trident deep into the earth, bringing forth a spring and the promise of maritime riches. Athena's response was to plant an olive tree next to the spring, symbolizing a future of peace and plenty.

The *poleis* were a response to population growth and competition for resources. Over time a fortified place of refuge evolved into a permanent storage center. At first this was controlled by an individual with the power of distribution, but as the cities grew into small states, a bourgeoisie of citizen-soldiers, or hoplites, formed, prepared to defend what they'd built in exchange for a say in how things were run. So began the process of political evolution from monarchy toward (for some) democracy.

Competition between *poleis* made for rapid military innovation. The Spartans perfected the phalanx, a lethally effective formation that involved serried ranks of long spears and locked shields, with armor protecting exposed body parts. Battles took place on specially selected flat ground, and resembled a pushing match. They ended when one party broke and ran. War was conducted according to Homeric rules: the fighting didn't begin until both sides were ready, and there were no surprises. Victory went to the most disciplined, which was usually Sparta.

Next came the trireme out of Corinth, though it was based on an earlier Phoenician design. This was a warship capable of reaching speeds of eleven knots and executing a U-turn in under a minute. With its three banks of oars, a trireme was "a kind of maritime guided missile" (Paul Cartledge), and it would dominate Mediterranean warfare for centuries to come.

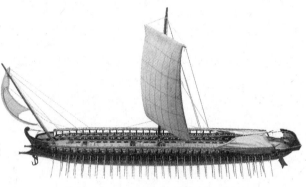

City-state super-weapon: the trireme

But the true genius of the Greeks was to create bodies such as the Delphic Oracle, which sat above the city-states, and the Olympic Games, which helped them to compete peacefully. The first Games were held at Olympia in the Peloponnese in the early eighth century BCE, and others joined them at Nemea, Isthmia, and Delphi, so that they became regular events, held annually or every two or four years. They were open to all Greeks, wherever they lived, so long as they were male (even the coaches were stripped to ensure they weren't proud mothers in disguise). These Games offered an annual alternative to war. They combined competition with diplomacy and were held under a strict truce that allowed athletes to travel and politicians to parley. While wrestlers grappled and javelins were hurled, alliances were made, new colonies planned, and tensions released.

The Games probably included a full recital of the *Iliad* across three evenings, perhaps as the soundtrack to the feast that followed the mass slaughter of one hundred bulls on the altar to Zeus. With its unmistakable message of Panhellenic cooperation and the disasters that would attend its breakdown, the recital would have powerfully underlined the very point of the Games.

Fair Play: Ancient and Modern

The Peloponnese (literally "island of Pelops") got its name from Prince Pelops of Lydia, in today's western Turkey. Legend has it that he came over to win the hand of Hippodameia, daughter of King Oenomaos, who ruled the land around what would become Olympia. The king challenged all suitors to a chariot race that he would always win. But Pelops procured his horses from Poseidon, then bribed the King's charioteer to replace his wheel axles with wax. Oenomaos was killed and Pelops won both his daughter and a kingdom. To celebrate, he held the first Games at Olympia.

Despite this rather ignoble origin story, the Games had a sound system for punishing cheats: they were fined, and the money spent on erecting *Zanes*. These were small statues dedicated to Zeus, with the cheater's name engraved on the plinth, his disgrace cast forever in stone.

Sparta

The film *300* vividly depicts the Spartans as the ultimate fighting machine, but their formidable reputation owed as much to their domestic arrangements as it did to foreign exploits. Having conquered and enslaved the native Achaeans of the Peloponnese, the invading Dorians found themselves vastly outnumbered by them. The Spartans (as they'd become) needed a social structure to keep these subjugated peoples in place.

City-states of the Peloponnese

According to the Spartans' foundation myth, a man named Lycurgus gave the Spartans their laws and system of government, perhaps in the ninth century BCE. This consisted of two kings, a House of Elders (the *Gerousia*, whose minimum age was sixty), and a hardened, militarized youth. Society was divided into three classes. At the top were the *spartiates*, Sparta's citizens, all male, who endured the tough *agoge* training regime between the ages of seven and twenty, when they joined a *syssition*. This was a kind of supper club, paid for with a monthly fee, whose fifteen members were deliberately undernourished on a diet that included black pig's blood broth.* *Spartiates* could marry at the age of twenty but not live with their wives for ten years after that. They remained on active service until they were sixty.

Next were the *perioikoi*, who were free but not citizens. These were often ex-*spartiates* unable to afford or cope with the *agoge*, and they existed as a sort of military reserve.

---

* The Sybarites quipped that the reason the Spartans didn't fear death was because it was preferable to a lifetime of their food.

At the bottom were the *helots*, or state-owned slaves, mainly made up of conquered Achaeans from Messenia and Laconia. Their lot was to produce food for the *spartiates* and be hunted annually by them for sport and training. The Spartans' enslavement of whole Greek tribes set them apart from the other city-states.

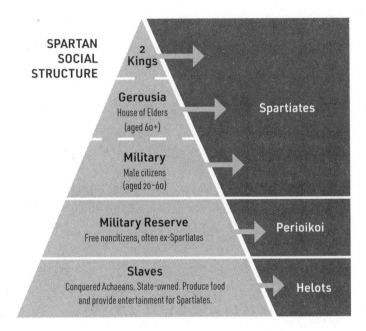

The Spartans weren't great writers, so much of what is known of them comes from their enemies, such as Aristotle, for instance, who considered them thugs. Did they really throw weak babies into a ravine in the Taygetos mountains? So far, archaeologists have only found adult remains there. Did they persecute the helots? Aristotle claimed they ritually declared war on them every year, but what evidence we have suggests that they treated them better than the Athenians treated their own slaves. Helots were allowed to keep half of what they produced, to marry, and to buy their freedom. Were Spartan women valued only as breeders of more and more Spartan men? Perhaps, but even so they were better off than most Greek women. They were educated, allowed to own property, and absolved from childbearing until their bodies were strong enough. On average they lived ten years longer than their counterparts in Athens.

Spartan Wit

Spartan smile: marble bust, possibly of King Leonidas, 490–480 BCE

In the archaeological museum in Sparta, the torso of a magnificent Spartan warrior is topped by a no less magnificent head, which is grinning from ear to ear. But was there room for humor in a state like Sparta? It's true that the Greek god of wine, Dionysus, had no festival there, but there was a temple to Gelos, god of laughter.

In fact the Spartans were famously witty. Socrates once said: "If you talk to any ordinary Spartan, he seems to be stupid. But eventually, like an expert marksman, he shoots in some brief remark that proves you to be only a child." And when Philip II of Macedon invaded southern Greece, he sent a threatening message to the Spartans asking if he should come as friend or foe. The reply was: "Neither." He then sent a nastier message to say that if he entered Laconia, he would raze Sparta. Another one-word message came back: "If."

Furthermore, the Greek word for Spartan, *lakon*, has given us the adjective *laconic*, meaning "dry or understated." *Attic* wit, on the other hand, was "subtle or delicate." Perhaps nothing defines difference like humor.

There was, however, a design flaw built into the Spartan system. The toughness of military training, the obstacles to family life, and heavy battle losses meant that true *spartiates* were in permanent decline. By Aristotle's day in the mid-fourth century BCE, citizenship had declined from nine thousand to one thousand, but the inflexibility of the Spartan social and political structure meant that any accommodation with the helot underclass was unthinkable.

THE CLASSICAL AGE (500–323 BCE)

It is called the Greek Miracle—two centuries of spectacular achievement in almost every field of human endeavor. These were the years when *demokratia* was established, first in Athens, then across the Greek city-states. This wasn't the representative democracy that we know today, but something more direct. Over those two hundred or so years, *demokratia* was born, peaked, declined, and was reinvented—though perhaps for another time, since by then tyranny was back. What the Greeks learned from that process is still of vital interest to us today.

The Path to Freedom

By the seventh century BCE, the Greek world consisted of more than a thousand city-states, run by elites who were against any form of democracy. In Athens, the ruling classes had taken over so much of the city's wealth that ordinary people began to rebel. In 594 BCE, a new ruler, Solon, began to think about how to run things differently.

For Solon, extremes of wealth were at the heart of the problem. "Nothing in excess" was another of the Delphic Oracle's dicta and Solon took it seriously. He abolished debt bondage and made public office dependent on means rather than birth, promoting the ambitious middle classes at the expense of the aristocracy. He allowed all citizens—even *thetes*, the poorest class of freemen—to attend the *ecclesia* (assembly) that made the city's laws, though they did not have the right to speak. Above all, he fostered *paideia* (education) as the way to spread *arete* (virtue) and inoculate the Athenians against tyranny. It was, he wrote, through ignorance that the people fell into "the bondage of the despot."

Yet the path to *demokratia* was not smooth. Solon was succeeded by the tyrant Peisistratus (561–527 BCE, off and on). Political reform ground to a halt, but Peisistratus continued Solon's good work in other areas. He kept most of his laws and solved Athens's notorious water problem by building wells and the West's first public fountain; land was redistributed and olive farmers subsidized. Peisistratus also understood the power of populist gestures. After his first exile, he dressed a tall woman in breastplate and helmet and made his triumphal reentry into the city in a golden chariot, with "Athena" by his side.

It was in 507 BCE, when Cleisthenes introduced the *deme* ("ward" or "district"), that true revolution came. The *deme* became the basis for a new concept of citizenship where the classes were mixed up so as to promote maximum—and fair—participation in the key functions of the *polis*: assemblies, religious festivals, law courts, and representation on the central council of five hundred. Citizens were chosen to serve by lot.

The Pnyx was the hill in Athens where the *ecclesia* was held, and the assembled citizens were now permitted to speak. There was room for about six thousand on it (perhaps a fifth of the total citizenry) and voting was by the simple raising of the right hand. To start with, it met once a month (more often later) and only rain could stop play—rain being a sign of divine disapproval. The *boule*, brainchild of Cleisthenes, was its steering committee, the body that prepared and instituted its laws.

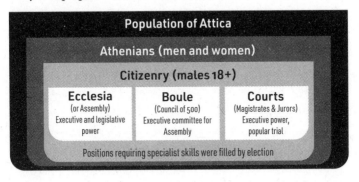

Population of Attica

Athenians (men and women)

Citizenry (males 18+)

Ecclesia	Boule	Courts
(or Assembly)	(Council of 500)	(Magistrates & Jurors)
Executive and legislative power	Executive committee for Assembly	Executive power, popular trial

Positions requiring specialist skills were filled by election

But, as Solon had known, *demokratia* only works if citizens understand why they're raising their hands. So an Athenian education had both to instruct and encourage informed participation. The system of *paideia* had long been teaching aristocratic children how to be model members of the *polis*. Now it was expanded to include the middle classes.

Paideia strove to promote *arete* ("virtue" or "excellence") in every area. It combined the study of the liberal arts and science with physical and moral education, imparted through music, poetry, and philosophy. Perhaps above all, it encouraged the mastery of rhetoric—a skill that was essential in a direct democracy.

Sparta was the only polis to have an official public education system. It, too, was designed to instill commitment to the *polis*, but its emphasis was on the martial. Spartan schooling did not encourage creative expression: there would never be a Spartan temple on a par with the Parthenon, nor a Spartan playwright to rival Aeschylus's genius.

Persian Wars

It was these two very different versions of the Greek *polis* that, early in the fifth century BCE, together faced the Persian invasions. Darius, the Persian "King of Kings," wanted to punish Athens for encouraging the Greek cities of Asia Minor to revolt against his rule. In 490 BCE he sent a task force across the Aegean sea to land at Marathon, just east of Athens. There it was defeated on the beach by the Athenian hoplites, and the Persians went home.

Pheidippides

Pheidippides (or perhaps Philippides) was the young *hemero-drome* ("day runner") who is said to have run three hundred miles from Athens to Sparta and back—then twenty-six miles from the battlefield of Marathon to Athens to bring news of victory. It may be the stuff of legend (and the Marathon-Athens leg of the legend was added much later) but it still quickens the pulse.

Pheidippides famously died on delivering his news—hardly surprising, given the 326 miles he'd covered in three days—but his heroism lived on to become inspiration for the first modern marathon race, introduced at the reborn Olympic games in 1896 and now run by millions across the world. He also inspired two twentieth-century Greek runners to athletic triumph at vital times in their nation's history. We'll come to them later.

Ten years later, the Persians, under Darius's son Xerxes, invaded again, this time with overwhelming force. In the first invasion, Sparta's forces had arrived too late to join the main action at Marathon. This time, King Leonidas led three hundred Spartan hoplites to defend the pass at Thermopylae, where they and others held off the Persians for three days before being betrayed by a local named Ephialtes, who showed the Persians a path to outflank them. Xerxes marched on to destroy Athens, including the Acropolis, and prepared to confront the Greek army at Corinth. But first he needed command of the sea. In a tactical masterstroke, the Athenian general Themistocles lured the huge Persian fleet into the straits of Salamis, where it was destroyed by the much smaller Greek one. A year later, the Persians were defeated at the battle of Plataea, and again they went home, this time for good.

Of the seven hundred or so *poleis* of the Greek heartland, only thirty-one had joined the coalition against the Persians. The Thebans, after fighting alongside the Spartans at Thermopylae, had swapped sides, and more Greeks fought with the Persians than against them. This meant that Athens and Sparta emerged from the wars with their reputations—and those of their very different systems of government—much boosted.

For the Athenians, victory over Persia vindicated a system that bound citizens from all classes to the *polis*. Before *demokratia*, it had been the cavalry of the aristocracy that had protected the people. Then it had been the farmer-citizen hoplites who won at Marathon. At Salamis, the very poorest class of citizen had rowed their triremes to victory.

The Spartan system, on the other hand, seemed to foster the iron discipline that made men stand firm at Thermopylae. Yet it was built around the enslavement of Greeks. Athenians might have admired its efficacy—and welcomed Sparta as an ally when expedient—but it was as much a threat as an object of emulation.

It was the Athenians who had produced perhaps the war's greatest leader. Themistocles had masterminded the brilliant subterfuge that lured the Persians to their destruction at Salamis. Then, in the decade between the two invasions, he had persuaded his fellow citizens to spend the dividend from their new silver mines wisely: on building more ships.

Oracles

Themistocles had a genius for interpreting the Delphic Oracle's answers to suit his purpose. When the Athenians asked how they should fend off the Persians, the priestess answered: "Only a wooden wall will save you." She might just as easily have been telling him to barricade the Acropolis, but Themistocles read it as "take to your ships." The Athenians went with that version and won at Salamis.

Her answers were famously ambiguous. Another leader weighing up whether to go to war was told: "You will go you will return never in war you will perish." The meaning hinges on the placement of a single punctuation mark.

At Delphi, the Oracle delivered her pronouncements on the seventh day of every month—seven being the sacred number for Apollo. Some said she was intoxicated by fumes seeping out of a geological vent below. Whether she was stoned or not, kings paid homage to her, and her strange utterances could alter the fate of empires.

Other oracles, like the one at Dodona in Epirus dedicated to Zeus and Dione, communicated via wind in the trees. At the museum in Ioannina there are lead tablets inscribed with the questions posed by visitors. One reads: "Lysanias asks Zeus Naios and Dione whether the baby Annyla is now bearing is really his."

King Croesus of Lydia is said to have tested the oracles by getting his men to ask each of them what he was doing at the precise time the question was asked. It was only Delphi that got it right: "eating lamb and tortoise stew."

When the oracles' answers got too baffling, the Greeks could always go to the nearest *Necromanteion*. There they'd consume a meal of pork, barley bread, and narcotics, before descending deep underground via stone steps and corridors to seek advice from the ancestors. Priests would often preside from above, suspended in midair by hidden machines.

With the Persians down but hardly out, the other city-states could choose either Athens or Sparta for protection. Two rival blocs, based broadly upon Dorian and Ionian tribal kinship, began to take shape. In the Peloponnese, with the exception of Argos, they looked to Sparta. North of the isthmus, with the exception of Thebes, and across most of the islands, they looked to Athens.

Aeschylus: dramatist and soldier

Aeschylus embodies the Golden Age when the Athenians "found themselves suddenly a great power. Not just in one field, but in everything they set their minds to" (Herodotus).

He was fifteen when Cleisthenes came to power, so witnessed firsthand the *deme* revolution that brought forth *demokratia* in Athens. He also experienced its apotheosis, fighting as a hoplite at Marathon (where his brother was killed), then at Salamis and Plataea. So he was well placed to sing its praises, and the few of his plays that still exist are hymns to freedom over despotism, order over chaos.

Aeschylus called his plays "slices from the banquet of Homer" and his best-known work, the *Oresteia* trilogy, depicts the Homeric movement from divine chaos to human order. The story opens with Agamemnon's return from Troy and his murder at the hands of his wife, Clytemnestra. This is her revenge for his sacrifice of their daughter Iphigenia to bring fair winds for his sea journey to Troy many years before. In the second play, their son Orestes kills his mother to avenge his father's murder. In the third, Orestes is pursued by terrifying goddesses (the Furies) as punishment for his matricide. Eventually, Orestes comes to Athens, where the city's patron goddess, Athena, summons a jury of twelve citizens. They acquit him and convert the Furies to *Eumenides* ("kindly ones"), forever after on the side of law and order over vendetta and chaos.

Tellingly, Aeschylus's gravestone at Gela made no mention of his plays:

> Beneath this stone lies Aeschylus, son of Euphorion,
> the Athenian, who perished in the wheat-bearing land
> of Gela; of his noble prowess the grove of Marathon
> can speak, and the long-haired Mede knows it well.

In the end, his commitment to the *polis* as a hoplite counted more than his genius as a playwright.

Aeschylus set Orestes's trial on the Areopagus, the big rock next to the Acropolis in the center of Athens. It was where the most serious cases were tried, such as homicide and the willful destruction of olive trees, which were sacred to Athena. It was also where, centuries later, St. Paul would preach Christianity to the bewildered Athenians.

Pericles

In the wake of victory over the Persians, a gifted orator named Pericles rose swiftly through the Athenian political ranks. By his mid-thirties he was an influential statesman, and he chose the Pnyx as his venue when he launched a bid to persuade his fellow citizens to adapt *demokratia* to the needs of a richer, more populous *demos*.

Pericles's reforms of 461 BCE placed more power in the hands of ordinary Athenians than ever before. Henceforth they would be paid from the city purse for jury service (and later, for attendance at the *ecclesia*, too), which meant that everyone could afford to participate. Pericles believed that the greatness of Athens came from every level of her talented citizenry, directed by education toward the common good. He dismissed individualists as *idiotes*.

Pericles delivers an oration on the Pnyx, 19th-century painting

Building the Parthenon

Today Pericles is remembered for the reconstruction of the Acropolis as much as for anything else. To oversee it, he appointed the sculptor Phidias (480–430 BCE), perhaps the greatest artist of the Classical Age. Phidias's statue of Zeus at Olympia, one of the Seven Wonders of the Ancient World, was so perfect that Zeus himself was said to have sent down a thunderbolt to show his satisfaction.

Work on the Acropolis started in 447 BCE, when Phidias carved the huge gold and ivory statue of Athena that the Parthenon was to house. The monumental entrance of the *Propylaea* and the Temple to Athena Nike (Athena Victory) followed, and the project was finished by 421 BCE.

Pericles came under fierce criticism from his opponents for the extravagance of the Parthenon construction. And Phidias's genius seems to have provoked its share of *phthonos* (envy). In 432 BCE, politically motivated charges of embezzlement were raised against him, and the *ecclesia* voted to imprison him. One of the greatest sculptors who ever lived may well have died behind bars.

For many in Athens, especially those of an oligarchic bent, Pericles's reforms could only lead to a dangerously powerful citizenry. Feelings ran high. Pericles's fellow-reformer Ephialtes was assassinated soon after the laws were enacted.

How many citizens were there? At the end of the Persian Wars there had been 30,000, out of a total population, including women and slaves, of perhaps 250,000. But in their aftermath Athens grew fast. In an effort to keep the city to a manageable size—and perhaps also to assuage the worries of the oligarchs—Pericles passed a law in 451 BCE that limited citizenship to those with two Athenian-born parents, rather than one.

The success of *demokratia* at home inspired Pericles and the Assembly to bind their allies abroad into a commonwealth of equals. In 478 BCE, Athens formed the Delian League of city-states, most of them across the Aegean and on the shores of Asia Minor. The League's main purpose was to continue the fight against Persia, and its members could either provide ships or money for the task. Most gave money.

Delos and the Delian League

The League's treasury was placed on the island of Delos, birthplace of Apollo and Artemis, and a place so sacred that even the Persians hadn't dared touch it.

Its Panhellenic sanctity made it a sensible place to put the money. Nobody seemed to mind that the treasurers (the *Hellenotamiae*) were all Athenian while the League was doing good things such as expelling the Persians from the rest of Greece, ridding the Aegean Sea of pirates, promoting trade, and introducing a common currency (the silver *tetradrachm*, bearing an image of Athena's wise owl). Versions of Athenian democracy spread to many of the League's city-states. But as the threat from Persia ebbed, members began asking why their contributions kept rising, and why so much was being spent on exclusively Athenian projects like the Parthenon.

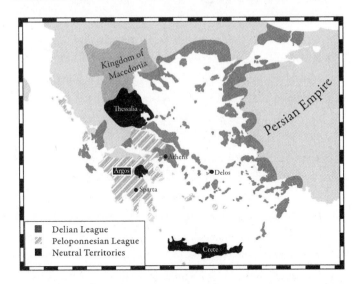

Athenian democracy began to take on an imperial hue. When Naxos and Thassos tried to leave the League, Athens responded by tearing down their city walls. In 454 BCE, Pericles moved the treasury to Athens, not only offending an important god but giving the lie to any pretense of democratic legitimacy.

The alliance with Sparta, which had never joined the League, also came under strain. In 465 BCE, Sparta requested Athenian help in subduing the latest helot revolt. Athens sent four thousand hoplites to the rebel base at the hill of Ithome overlooking Messene, but their behavior soon led the Spartans to suspect that they were about to switch sides and support the slaves. They were sent home. It was a very public insult to Athenian *philotimo*, and it could only end one way.

Philotimo

Philotimo, literally "love of honor," is still alive and well in Greece today. It embraces a complicated set of values with roots in the ancient world.

In a culture that set little store by the afterlife, *kleos* was the kind of everlasting glory, mainly earned on the battlefield, that would be celebrated by the bards for centuries after an individual's demise.

Timi was the honor paid to you in your lifetime, again usually won in battle, again usually earned by men.

Arete underpinned all the other virtues and was the aim of ancient Greek education: a blend of knowledge, physical prowess, courage, and, again, success in battle.

The cautionary antithesis to the qualities above was *aidos*: the terrible shame endured as a result of cowardice and failure. Success mattered in Athens.

In *Song of Wrath* (2010), his brilliant account of the Peloponnesian War, J. E. Lendon argues that *philotimo* rather than territorial gain was the main driver of events. The humiliation of the enemy was pretty much as important as his defeat.

As for women, they had to rely on *dolos*, meaning guile or trickery. Pandora is the embodiment of *dolos*, using beauty, lies, and crafty words to seduce men and empty their pockets. Her name translates as "all the gifts" because every Olympian god donated something to her creation.

The Peloponnesian War

Like the World Wars of the twentieth century, the murderous nearly thirty-year war between Athens and Sparta changed everything. It was sparked by the usual mix of *hubris*, envy, and insults to honor, but at its heart was the clash of two opposing versions of government. In the end, Spartan oligarchy would triumph over Athenian democracy (though only for a time). By then both sides were exhausted caricatures of what they'd once been. Sparta would tarnish the glories of Thermopylae and Plataea by calling on the Persians for help, while Athenian democracy would degrade into populism.

The war began well for Athens. Pericles persuaded his fellow citizens to abandon their crops and withdraw within the city walls rather than face the Spartan hoplites in battle. Athenian naval supremacy ensured the city was kept supplied by sea while its triremes harassed the Peloponnesian coastline.

The historian Thucydides relates Pericles's famous funeral speech, in which he honored the warriors slain in 431 BCE, the first year of the war. It gives us some idea of the level of Athenian self-confidence at this time.

Our government does not copy our neighbors, but is an example to them.... For we have a peculiar power of thinking before we act, and of acting, too, whereas other men are courageous from ignorance but hesitate upon reflection.... I say that Athens is the school of Hellas, and that the individual Athenian seems to have the power of adapting himself to the most varied forms of action with the utmost versatility and grace....

The speech was delivered to the grieving women of Athens (for once allowed out in public) who had lost fathers, sons, and brothers in the war. Pericles told them that their pain was worth it for the glory of Athens, the school of Hellas. Yet these losses were nothing against what was to come.

A year later, the overcrowded city was visited by a plague—probably typhus—killing a third of the population, including Pericles himself. Thucydides also caught it, but survived to witness the total breakdown of Athenian order:

> The calamity that weighed upon them was so overpowering that men, not knowing where to turn, grew reckless of all law, human and divine.

This recklessness began to infect Athenian politics, as a new breed of populists fed off the fear and anger of ordinary citizens. In 427 BCE, the city of Mytilene on Lesbos rose in revolt against Athens, expecting Sparta's backing. But the Spartans didn't show up and the city was forced to surrender. Whipped into a frenzy by the demagogue Cleon, the Assembly voted to slaughter all Mytilene's men and enslave its women and children, immediately dispatching a trireme across the Aegean for the purpose. The next day, realizing the folly of their decision, they sent another ship to revoke the order. The oarsmen rowed night and day, arriving just as the sentence was being read out on the beach. The Mytileneans were saved only by a fair wind.

In 421 BCE, the Peace of Nicias brought the first part of the war to an end, with honors roughly even. But Pericles seemed to have taken all residue of Athenian wisdom with him to the grave, as his city's cherished democracy moved toward something more extreme.

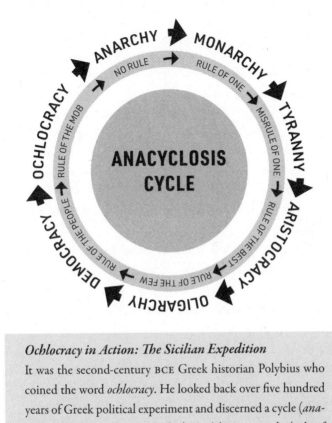

ANARCHY
NO RULE

MONARCHY
RULE OF ONE

TYRANNY
MISRULE OF ONE

ARISTOCRACY
RULE OF THE BEST

OLIGARCHY
RULE OF THE FEW

DEMOCRACY
RULE OF THE PEOPLE

OCHLOCRACY
RULE OF THE MOB

ANACYCLOSIS CYCLE

Ochlocracy in Action: The Sicilian Expedition

It was the second-century BCE Greek historian Polybius who coined the word *ochlocracy*. He looked back over five hundred years of Greek political experiment and discerned a cycle (*anacyclosis*) that went from *anarchy* (no rule) to *monarchy* (rule of the one) to *aristocracy* (rule of the best) to *oligarchy* (rule of the few) to *democracy* (rule of the people). Ochlocracy (rule of the mob) followed when a dissatisfied majority looked to populist demagogues for answers.

What happened next in the Peloponnesian War comes straight out of the Polybius playbook. By 415 BCE, Athens and Sparta had been at peace for six years, but it was an uneasy truce. When the opportunity arose for the Athenians to support a local revolt against the pro-Sparta rulers of Syracuse on Sicily, the Assembly was split between a "peace party," led by Nicias, and one keen to renew the war, led by Alcibiades. Stoked up by Alcibiades, the Assembly voted to send a large-scale expedition to Syracuse. It was a risky move: if it failed, Athens would struggle to defend herself at home.

It failed disastrously. From the start, the leadership was divided, with both Nicias and Alcibiades part of the command. Then Alcibiades defected to Sparta, which set about reinforcing the Syracusans. The Athenian army and fleet were virtually annihilated. It was the turning point of the whole war, and though Athens continued the fight for another decade, she was fatally weakened.

By the end, Athens was under more or less permanent siege. Sparta had teamed up with the old enemy, Persia, to build a fleet large enough to blockade the city by sea. Thus starved, the Athenians finally surrendered in 404 BCE.

Aftermath

Sparta refrained from razing Athens to the ground. Instead, it tore down her walls and imposed a brutal oligarchic regime.

The Thirty Tyrants, as they were called, didn't last long. By 403 BCE, democracy was back and the Athenians were pondering how to improve it. To counter the power of unscrupulous demagogues like Cleon, they set up a new body, chosen by lot, that would scrutinize the decisions of the Assembly. Athenian democracy wasn't going into reverse; it was being retooled for acceleration.

The Trial of Socrates

The trial of the seventy-year-old Socrates in 399 BCE bears witness to the febrile atmosphere in Athens in the wake of defeat, as people sought answers to the question of what had gone wrong. The philosopher was charged with two crimes:

impiety against the gods, and corruption of the youth of Athens. To Athenians who believed that freedom had been taken too far, the charges had merit.

Socrates presented himself as the "gadfly of Athens," stinging its populace into confronting the decay of their democracy. An unmistakable presence on the city's streets, he would stop passers-by to question them. Many thought he was setting the younger generation against its elders, hence the accusation of corrupting the youth.

As for impiety against the gods, recent defeat against the Spartans helped make the charge stick. It must have seemed self-evident to many among the five-hundred-strong, randomly selected jury that the gods had withdrawn their support. And hadn't Socrates added his own private deities to the traditional Athenian pantheon? Even so, the jury's decision to impose the death sentence speaks of an anxious, insecure society still in thrall to the mob— exactly what the Athenians were trying to move away from.

Meanwhile Sparta, having won the war, saw no reason not to take over the wider Athenian empire, imposing its own oligarchic style of rule wherever it could. But taking on the mantle of Athens meant assuming its commitments too, and it soon found itself fighting another war against Persia (400–387 BCE) in support of the Greek cities of Asia Minor.

The results of Spartan hubris were not long in coming. In 395 BCE, all the other big city-states (Thebes, Corinth, Athens, and Argos) joined against it, backed by a Persian king only too delighted to exploit Greek division for his own ends. But at the last moment, the Persians changed sides. A humiliating King's Peace was imposed, which restored Persian control over the Greek cities of Asia Minor and undid the gains of all the Persian wars fought previously. Yet despite the war's outcome, the other city-states had sensed Spartan weakness. They just needed a leader with the talent to exploit it.

Thebes and the End of Spartan Supremacy

Epaminondas of Thebes was that man. Thebes was among the oldest of the Greek city-states. It proudly traced its foundation to Cadmus, first of the mythical "heroes," and its acropolis, the Cadmeia, was named for him. Historically it had always been ruled by a tyrant or oligarchy, and had remained loyal to Sparta throughout the Peloponnesian War. But the Thebans had felt short-changed after the war was over. They had not been granted the expected territory as a reward for their support, and to their annoyance Sparta had allowed their old rival, Athens, to survive. Thus alienated, they had joined the alliance against Sparta. Now, with the alliance defeated, Sparta broke the terms of the King's Peace by sending a garrison to occupy the Cadmeia, an act as sacrilegious as it was illegal.

Epaminondas, a Theban statesman and veteran of the war, seized his chance. He assembled a fighting force consisting of Thebans exiled in Athens (who'd embraced the *demokratia* they found there) and young men within the city, then marched on the Cadmeia to expel the Spartans.

> The war that broke down the pretensions of Sparta, and put an end to her supremacy by land and sea, began from that night.
>
> Plutarch

In 378 BCE, under the leadership of Epaminondas, Thebes became a democracy for the first time. With a newly reformed army, it now set about defeating Sparta and furthering the cause of democracy across Greece. Seven years later, at the Battle of

Leuctra, Epaminondas did the unthinkable: he won. The myth of Spartan invincibility was broken forever.

Epaminondas

Epaminondas did more to reshape the political map of Greece than anyone until Philip of Macedon. For the sixteenth-century French philosopher Michel de Montaigne, he was one of the "three worthiest and most excellent men who had ever lived." Such praise rests above all on two achievements: his defeat of Sparta and the liberation of its helots.

In defeating a larger Spartan army at Leuctra, in 371 BCE, Epaminondas turned traditional hoplite tactics on their head. Instead of placing his best troops on the right of the line, he put them on the left, and in ranks fifty deep instead of the normal twelve. Then he ordered the less experienced men on the right to "avoid battle and withdraw gradually during the enemy's attack" (Xenophon). By concentrating overwhelming force against an enemy line that was already turning, he was able to roll it up from the flank.

Epaminondas owed part of his success to an elite force within the Theban army as good as any produced by the Spartan *agoge*. This was the Sacred Band: a body of 300 hoplites made up of 150 pairs of older and younger male lovers. It was their role in preventing encirclement by the much larger Spartan army that won the day at Leuctra.

But Epaminondas was more than just a brilliant military tactician. He understood that Sparta's citizen army was only able to devote itself to fighting because slaves did everything else. By freeing the Messenians and then helping them build the city stronghold of Messene, Epaminondas undermined Sparta's entire way of life.

It was at Mantinea in 362 BCE, the biggest hoplite battle in Greek history, that Epaminondas won his greatest victory and permanently brought an end to Spartan preeminence. It was his coup de grâce: he died from his wounds soon afterward.

Epaminondas seems to have been an ascetic figure, without vanity and personally incorruptible. His reshaping of Greece—not just in defeating Sparta but in promoting democracy wherever he could—appears to have been driven less by personal ambition than by a sense of moral duty. He deserves to be remembered more than he is.

In 378 BCE, the same year it became a democracy, Thebes joined a new Athenian league. This one seemed to have learned the lessons from the ill-fated Delian one of a century before. There would be no forced tribute and the autonomy of each member would be respected. Soon its membership grew to seventy-five, and many of them were democracies.

This development made a major contribution toward making the second quarter of the fourth century BCE *the golden age of ancient Greek democracy*.

Paul Cartledge, *Democracy: A Life* (author's emphasis)

The alliance didn't last long. Relations between Athens and Thebes soon deteriorated, and by mid-century many of the islands had severed connections with the League and jettisoned their democratic governments.

Yet within Athens itself, the search for a better way to rule continued unabated. For the city's great minds, nothing was off the table. Xenophon wanted constitutional monarchy: a king ruling with the advice, consent, and support of the aristocracy. Isocrates looked to education to build an entire population of *philosophoi* able to withstand the lies of demagogues. Plato advocated a strange and brutal utopia that was at once reactionary and ahead of its time.

Plato's Republic

Perhaps no other book has divided historical opinion as deeply as Plato's *Republic*. For some it's the bracing common sense that once inspired British boarding schools; for others, the terrifying tool kit for a brave new world. Rousseau, presiding spirit of the French Revolution, considered it "the most beautiful educational treatise ever written."

Plato believed in a meritocracy of intellect drawn from every section of society, formed by natural ability and perfected through education. Mankind, he thought, was naturally divided into gold (the "guardians" of the Republic), silver (the wealth creators), and bronze (farmers and artisans). Since talent was not always inherited, society had to undergo a continual process of re-sorting.

Some of Plato's ideas—about communal childrearing or the "noble lie" of state propaganda—are repugnant to us today. Others, such as his insistence on social mobility and equality between men and women, strike us as ahead of his time. And his most profound message still resonates: of the vital importance of education to the health and stability of the community.

Aristotle, one of Plato's pupils, tasked his students with compiling a database of political systems tried by city-states so far. The result was the chart below—six ways in which the *poleis* had ruled themselves, categorized according to who ruled, and for the benefit of whom. In the upper row are the three "true" forms of government; in the second the specific form of corruption to which each was vulnerable. Aristotle blamed Athens's defeat in the Peloponnesian War on the extreme nature of its democracy. For him, democracy itself was a distortion of the *polity* (top right) that he believed gave the best chance of ruling in the interests of most people for the longest possible duration.

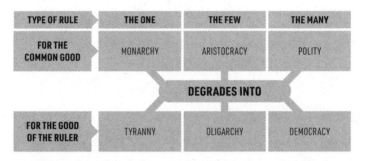

TYPE OF RULE	THE ONE	THE FEW	THE MANY
FOR THE COMMON GOOD	MONARCHY	ARISTOCRACY	POLITY
DEGRADES INTO			
FOR THE GOOD OF THE RULER	TYRANNY	OLIGARCHY	DEMOCRACY

Aristotle's Polity

Aristotle believed that the *polis* represented the ideal community for government—politics being literally "matters pertaining to the *polis*." The best ways to rule the *polis* were via an enlightened monarchy or an aristocracy, but these had a habit of degrading into tyrannies and oligarchies. So he turned to a more limited form of the democracy advocated by Cleisthenes and Pericles. His "polity" mixed the direct participation of citizens (excluding women) with election for roles that required technical expertise (e.g., in military or financial matters). The whole was underpinned by four principles that would protect it from populist demagogues:

MODERATION. Solon's avoidance of extremes, particularly in wealth and individual expression. As the Delphic Oracle had prescribed: "Nothing in excess."

A STRONG MIDDLE CLASS to act as a balance between the tyranny of the poor (what democracy risked becoming) and the tyranny of the rich (the main pitfall of oligarchy). In Aristotle's words: "The great preserving principle that the loyal citizens should be stronger in number than the disloyal."

A LEGAL SYSTEM that could withstand changes in the political climate: "as man is the best of animals when perfected, so he is the worst of all when sundered from law and justice." Laws should be adapted to suit changing conditions, but their purpose was to uphold the constitution, and this should change only rarely.

EDUCATION (*paideia*) to cultivate virtue (*arete*) and fit citizens for participation in the government of the polis and imbue them with law-abidingness (*eunomia*).

For Aristotle, the key to freedom was direct participation in the government of the *polis*—for all to rule and be ruled in turn. But such unmediated democracy could only be as good as the moral health of its participants. Provided they were properly educated toward *arete*, Aristotle believed that the people were *as good as or better than* any elite claiming to rule in their interest.

Philip of Macedon

While all this intellectual energy was pulsing through Athens, the world outside its walls was bleeding after decades of war. Brigandry was rife across the mainland, and fields were being left unharvested. Even in Athens itself, the law courts ceased to function because there wasn't enough money to pay the jurors.

Uncertainty and confusion had gained ground, being tenfold greater throughout the length and breadth of Hellas.

Xenophon on Greece after Mantinea (362 BCE)

Greeks began to look for a strongman to restore order. Philip II of Macedon (382–336 BCE) had already transformed his northern kingdom into a rich and expanding nation with a formidable army. In many ways he seemed to be one of them: his capital, Pella, was laid out as a Greek city; he spoke a form of Greek; and he claimed ancestry from the Argead dynasty of Argos.

In 346 BCE, the ageing philosopher Isocrates addressed Philip from Athens. It was thirty-five years since he had called on the Athenians to lead a Panhellenic crusade against Persia. Now, in more desperate times, he turned to the warriors of Macedon. Unless they stepped in, there'd be anarchy:

> If you undertake to conquer the whole empire of the [Persian] king, you will settle in permanent abodes those who now . . . are wandering from place to place and committing outrages on whomsoever they encounter. If we do not stop these men from banding together . . . they will grow before we know it into so great a multitude as to be a terror.

To other Greeks, though, Philip's brand of absolute rule was exactly what they had escaped from. In 340 BCE, the great statesman Demosthenes persuaded the Assembly to break their treaty with him. The result, in 338 BCE, was the Battle of Chaeronea, in which Athens and a combination of city-states (not including Sparta) were pulverized by the phalanxes of Philip's army.

Philip formed the defeated into the League of Corinth and declared himself commander of a Panhellenic war against the Persian empire. Shortly afterward, he was assassinated.

The End of Democracy
True *demokratia* came to an end in Greece in 338 BCE. It had had

a good run: more than two hundred years. In Athens it had been battered by war, defeat, famine, plague, coup—even the destruction of the entire city by the Persians—yet only once had it succumbed to tyranny, and then not for long. Democracy had raised the city to its highest peaks of wealth and influence. Right to the end, as tyranny hammered at the gates, Athenians were battling to repair it. It's hard to say the same of many of our democracies today.

A certain way of thinking died with *demokratia*. Aristotle was among the last Greek philosophers to see the good life as dependent on the political context in which it was lived. The new generation brought philosophers such as Diogenes the Cynic, who slept in a jar and sought not to reform the *polis* but to escape from it. For men like him there could be no social or political solution, only a personal one. A few centuries later, as we shall see, such ideas would segue neatly into the new religion of Christianity.

Alexander

Alexander's fame has rolled down the centuries, gathering myth along the way. He was a brilliant leader, loved by his men, whose every battle is still studied at West Point and Sandhurst. He was

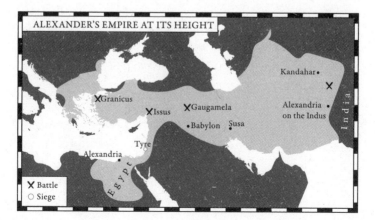

ALEXANDER'S EMPIRE AT ITS HEIGHT

Kandahar
Granicus
Issus   Gaugamela
Babylon   Susa
Alexandria
on the Indus
India
Tyre
Alexandria
Egypt
X Battle
○ Siege

intelligent, curious, and open to learning from those he conquered. The cities he founded stretched from Egypt to Afghanistan; his legacy was the fabulous Hellenistic age.

Was he visionary or conquistador? Perhaps both. Had he lived longer, his reputation might not have survived the growing megalomania and paranoia of his final years, or the alcohol-fueled rages, during one of which he murdered Cleitus, the friend who had once saved his life in battle.

There is also his failure to name a successor. The story goes that, when asked on his deathbed to whom the empire should pass, he replied: "To the strongest." Not helpful in a room full of alpha males. The result was fifty more years of war.

Alexander the Greek?

Two European countries claim Alexander as their own, so it's worth asking the question. But what was it to be Greek in an age before nations had been invented? For Herodotus, it was sharing a language, religion, blood, and way of life. Alexander was from Macedonia, but he spoke Greek, worshipped Greek gods, and had Greek blood in his veins via his mother, Olympias, whose family was from Epirus.

Yet could a man who claimed descent from Zeus-Ammon (a hybrid of Greek and Egyptian deities) really be said to subscribe to the Greek way of life? After all, it was a way of life that put the citizens of the *polis*, not their gods, at its center.

It isn't clear how much *demokratia* Alexander intended for his vast empire, stretching from Pella to the Punjab. During the eleven-year campaign that forged it, he is said to have slept with his tutor Aristotle's copy of Homer's epic poems under his pillow. But did he draw inspiration from Aristotle or from Homer? From the violent heroism of Achilles or Odysseus's quest for the just and simple life? Was he persuaded by Aristotle's *polity* or by the enlightened monarchy the philosopher had seen as the (albeit impossible) ideal?

We will never know exactly what Alexander thought about *demokratia* or what his long-term plans were for the empire. But it's certainly true that he wanted not just to subjugate the world but to teach it to be Greek.

It was an extraordinary campaign by any standards, up there with anything that Caesar or Napoleon did. The Greek city-states joined it only reluctantly, sending a mere seven thousand infantry and six hundred cavalry. They had not forgiven Alexander for the destruction of Thebes, which had risen against the young king at his accession. Sparta abstained altogether.

With an army of thirty-five thousand, Alexander marched first to Troy, following Xerxes's invasion route of 480 BCE. It was an act of emphatically Greek revenge. In 334 BCE, he defeated the local satraps sent to stop him at Granicus in northern Anatolia, and moved on to plunder the treasury at Sardis, the regional capital. Thus enriched, and with his army reinforced by the Greeks of Asia Minor, he marched east. In 333 BCE, the Persian Emperor Darius met him at Issus, north of Palestine, with a huge army of perhaps four hundred thousand. Again, the Persians were defeated, with Darius himself narrowly escaping death at the point of Alexander's spear.

Alexander the Winner of Battles
Alexander was a superb military tactician: a brilliant reader of terrain and an ingenious commander in the field. Like Napoleon and Julius Caesar, he had something else, too: the mix of personal courage and leadership that persuades men to lay down their lives.

The Greek phalanx had been around for centuries. What Alexander did was to equip it with much longer spears (*sarissa*) that could pin down the massed infantry of Darius while cavalry attacked from the side or behind. These cavalrymen were called the Companions (*hetairoi*) and they would charge in wedge formation with Alexander at their head.

In battle, the Companions would be the hammer to the infantry's anvil. It was their shock tactics that very nearly cost Darius his life at Issus. As for Alexander, it seems amazing that he lived as long as he did.

At Tyre in 332 BCE, Alexander turned tyrant to achieve his aims, slaughtering all the city's inhabitants after a seven-month siege. He then moved south into Egypt, traveling far into the desert to learn from the oracle at Siwah that he was the son of Zeus-Ammon. Thus deified, he returned to found the city of Alexandria and lay the foundations for the great age to follow.

The following year, he again faced overwhelming odds, at the battle of Gaugamela in today's Iraq. Seeing off the fearsome scythe-bearing chariots of the Persians, he marched on to take Babylon, then Susa, then the Persian capital, Persepolis, which he largely razed to the ground.

The Susa Weddings

Six years later, Alexander would return to Susa to oversee the mass wedding of Macedonian officers to noble Persian women. This exercise was supposed to send out a message of cultural fusion between erstwhile enemies. Alexander himself married Darius's eldest daughter, Stateira, which meant that he could thenceforth declare himself King of Kings and march off with a combined Greek-Persian army to conquer the world. Hephaestion, his close friend and commander of the Companions, married Stateira's sister and so became Alexander's brother-in-law.

Alexander seems to have hoped that the offspring of this elite would provide a new ruling class combining the best in Greek and Persian character. It didn't happen. Straight after his death, all the Macedonians bar one divorced their Persian wives.

After a grueling decade-long campaign had taken it all the way to the Punjab, Alexander's army refused to go further. Like Achilles, he took to his tent to sulk, before eventually giving in. His undefeated army turned around and made for home.

Alexander returned to Babylon where, after a particularly heavy night of drinking, he died in 323 BCE at the age of just thirty-two. Darius's mother, Sisygambis, is said to have retired to her rooms and starved herself to death on hearing the news.

Alexander's Macedonian generals had only ever been there for the booty. Conquistadors to a man, they not only divorced their wives but expelled all Persians from their midst, then set about carving their own empires out of the huge landmass to which Alexander had left no heir. Meanwhile, the Greeks back home broke out in rebellion.

Alexander's successors had the resources to quash all uprisings and still have some left over to fight among themselves. An estimated 180,000 talents (about $100 billion in today's money) had been extracted from the Persian Empire, perhaps the greatest transfer of wealth by conquest ever seen.

This wealth created the glory of the Hellenistic Age.

THE HELLENISTIC AGE (323–30 BCE)

> We the Alexandrians, the Antiochenes, the Seleucians,
> and the numerous
> other Hellenes of Egypt and Syria,
> and those in Media, and those in Persia, and so many others.
> With their extended dominions,
> And the diverse endeavours towards judicious adaptations.
> And the Greek *koine* language
> All the way to Bactria we carried it, to the peoples of India.
>
> C. P. Cavafy (1863–1933), "In the year 200 BC"

In 1961, Mohammad Zahir Shah, last king of Afghanistan, was out hunting high in the mountains of the Hindu Kush when he came across man-made stones peeping from the barren earth.

The Shah had discovered Ai-Khanoum, an eastern outpost of a Greek civilization that, "in the year 200 BC," had stretched as far west as Marseilles. The city boasted a six-thousand-seat theater, a gymnasium, temples, and an agora. Ai-Khanoum was on the doorstep of two other great civilizations: the Buddhist Maurya Empire of India and the Confucian Han of China. Greek coins decorated with Hindu deities and Buddhas in Hellenic apparel bear witness to cultural cross-fertilization, or "judicious adaptations," as Cavafy put it.

The three cultures differed in their understanding of what made for human happiness. For the Buddhists, it was the inner stillness that stemmed from an absence of desire. For followers of Confucius, it was obedience to a higher order. For Greeks, happiness came from participation—the exercise of man's inborn social and linguistic gifts—and the perfect venue for this, as Aristotle had argued, was the *polis*. Ai-Khanoum and the many other cities founded by Alexander were the lymph nodes of a new Hellenistic world order.

Carved onto the grave of Ai-Khanoum's founder, Kineas, were the maxims of the oracle of Delphi, which had been proffering advice to the Greek world since time immemorial. Most famous of these was "Know thyself." People have argued over its meaning, but the American author and poet Maya Angelou (née Johnson: she married a Greek sailor) has given perhaps the most compelling interpretation:

> If you don't know where you've come from, you don't know where you're going.

The Greeks who filled Alexander's empire to create the Hellenistic Age knew where they'd come from: the *polis*. In the next phase of the Greek story, a new kind of *polis* would blossom across the Hellenistic world, judiciously adapted, certainly, but still vibrant.

The Inhabited World

The Hellenistic Age spanned three centuries, from the death of Alexander to the Roman defeat of Ptolemaic Egypt and the suicide of its queen, Cleopatra, in 30 BCE. For many, it was a good time to be Greek. A new word came into being: *oecumene*. It meant the "inhabited world," and to the Greeks who measured, mapped, and largely ran it, this was *their* world.

If a Greek of the third century BCE had traveled to the city of Kandahar (named for Alexander) in Afghanistan, he'd have found the edicts of the great Indian Emperor Ashoka carved in stone—in Greek. A century later, if one of his ancestors had traveled even further east—to Sagala in the Punjab—he'd have reached the capital of the Kingdom of Menander I (ruled 165–130

BCE), an Indo-Greek potentate who'd converted to Buddhism. The language of Menander's administration was Greek and his coins were embossed with images of Athena.

At Gandhara in today's Pakistan, there are statues from as late as the second century CE showing the Buddha under the protection of Heracles. To this day, a city in Gujarat, far down the west coast of India, bears the name Junadagh—originally Yonadagh or "city of the Greeks" (*Yona* is a transliteration of Ionians). Even further south, in Sri Lanka, the *Mahavamasa*, a Buddhist text dating from the fifth century, refers to Greek missionaries helping to spread the word of the Buddha.

Buddha with Hellenic toga and topknot, Gandhara, Pakistan c. 1st to 2nd century CE

Greek thought had taken wing and flown to the outer reaches of the world, and it was all thanks to Alexander. Greek philosophers could swap ideas with Buddhist yogis and Persian magi. The fruits of this exchange would benefit the Mongols, the Abbasid Caliphs, and the Renaissance scholar princes of the future. It would benefit us all.

Fifty Years of War

First, though, more war—fifty years of it. After Alexander's death, the main rivals for the succession met at Babylon to try to sort things out calmly. It didn't work. Gradually the many became the few in a game of unremitting violence in which only two claimants

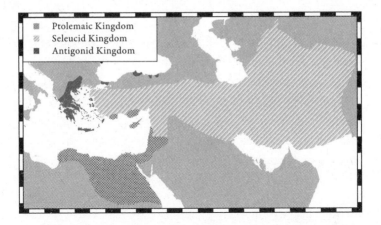

were fortunate enough to die in their beds. Huge armies and their elephants lumbered back and forth across Asia until just three dynasties remained: the Ptolemies in Egypt and southern Syria; the Seleucids, who ruled vast territories stretching east as far as India; and the Antigonids in Macedon and most of the Greece mainland. Within two generations, they'd all be related to one another and trapped in a gory cycle of sex, murder, and power politics. For now, though, a sort of status quo was established.

Alexander had founded at least a dozen cities. His successors, foremost among them the Seleucids, would found many more. For the native Greeks, whose land had never fully recovered from the Peloponnesian Wars, the opportunity was too good to miss. They emigrated to this new world in the tens of thousands. Unlike the Europeans who would colonize the Americas two millennia later, the Greeks were following a long-established tradition. For centuries they had been founding settlements, from Marseilles to Olbia at the mouth of the Bug River, in Ukraine, bringing their culture and laws with them. They knew what they were doing.

How did these settlers, raised in the republican tradition of the *polis*, get along among these absolute monarchies?

Pragmatically, it seems. The Hellenistic kings were no democrats, but they needed skilled administrators and governors. Soon an elite of Greek civil servants emerged: talented men who could always leave to serve another court if they weren't happy.

Lower down the social scale, ordinary citizens were happy to obey their new rulers, provided they could run their own affairs. Old and new *poleis* were permitted their own assemblies, agoras, theaters, and gymnasia, as long as they accepted that *demokratia* would travel no further than the city walls.

Hippodamus of Miletus (498–408 BCE)

Many of the new cities were laid out according to the grid system that had been perfected by Hippodamus of Miletus some two centuries before. Like Aristotle, Hippodamus had combined political theory with a host of other interests, including mathematics, meteorology, and medicine. His genius was to design cities in which the principles of *demokratia* could flourish. The great Hellenistic cities of Alexandria, Halicarnassus, and Antioch were all laid out according to the Hippodamian template, and his ideas were strong enough to last right through the Hellenistic and Roman periods.

The model city was designed for a maximum of fifty thousand citizens (Aristotle had preferred ten thousand as the maximum for his *polity*) and it was divided into space for the sacred, the public, and the private. Sacred and public spaces would coexist within a large central area, or agora, to which the city's districts of two-story private housing would have equal and easy access, via a grid plan of broad, straight streets.

Good examples of Hippodamian city layout can still be seen at two sites in mainland Greece: at Messene (built by

> Epaminondas in 369 BCE) in the Peloponnese, and Kassope
> in Epirus, whose facilities seem to have included two theaters
> and a thirty-one-bedroom hotel.

The citizens of these new Hellenistic *poleis* did not enjoy the same *demokratia* as their ancestors in classical times. Public offices were filled more by election than lottery, and some roles, like the generalships, weren't put to the vote at all. What was the point when foreign policy was decided by kings, and it was mercenaries rather than citizen-soldiers who fought the battles, usually in distant lands? It's not for nothing that the cult of Tyche, goddess of fortune, gained new followers at this time. The world outside the city walls was an unpredictable place, or at least one beyond the control of ordinary people.

Yet, especially in Greece and Anatolia, the *poleis* clung on to what they could of the old freedoms. They still had their assemblies and made their own laws. Some even struck their own coinage. And citizens were still empowered to honor the best among them for services to the *polis*:

> It has been resolved by the *Boule* and the People that Sotas, son
> of Lykos, be praised for his bravery . . . and that he be crowned
> with a wreath of palm leaves in the theatre during the tragic
> contest at the next Dionysia.
>
> > Priene, western Anatolia, early third century BCE

As a rule, the further east you went, the less *demokratia* there was. Around 250 BCE, the Parthian Empire established itself in modern Iran, driving a wedge between the Greeks in the Hindu Kush and those around the Mediterranean, and fraying still further the threads of Hellenic identity.

By the second century BCE, the great centers of Greek culture all bordered the Mediterranean: Alexandria, Antioch, Pergamum, and Athens. Travel between them was easy, and wherever they went Greeks found a recognizable language, legal code, and city layout, with temples dedicated to gods they knew well. There was even something close to an international currency.

On mainland Greece, ruled by the Antigonid dynasty from their power base in Macedon, the *poleis* tried to reestablish some control over their foreign affairs, forming federations to resist autocratic rule. The most successful were the Achaean and Aetolian Leagues.

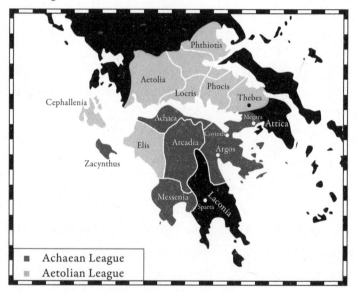

The Achaean League, based in the Peloponnese, became the main rival to Antigonid Macedon. It was controlled by an elite class of wealthy landowners, yet according to the Greek political scientist Polybius (of whom more later) it brought peace, and perhaps even a first sense of Greek nationhood:

> In the past, many have tried to unite the Peloponnesians. . . .
> But in my own time this object has been so much advanced
> and so far attained that . . . almost the whole Peloponnese only
> narrowly falls short of being one city.

Athens chose not to join any league. The city was now a fashionable center of philosophy and higher education, its loss of autonomy after 321 BCE offset by new wealth and luxury. The Assembly still gathered but only the rich took part, and they were happy to vote up statues to their Antigonid overlords. Yet it seems that democracy was still working at some level. New *demes*, adding to the city's existing total of 139, were being created right up to 126 BCE.

Sparta, too, had remained aloof from the leagues. By the mid-third century BCE, it had lost Messenia, abandoned the military training regime of the *agoge*, and was reduced to 700 families, of whom only about 100 owned land. Two kings, Agis IV and Cleomenes III, tried to stop the rot. They redistributed the land, restored the *agoge* and the laws of Lycurgus, and even permitted the fringe class of *perioikoi* (free men, but not citizens) to become full-fledged *spartiates*.

The reforms worked, and soon enough Sparta began to throw its weight around. After a series of victories against its neighbors, it came up against the Achaean League, whose leaders panicked and turned to Macedon for help. At the Battle of Sellasia (222 BCE), Antigonus Doson of Macedon and the Achaeans annihilated the Spartan army. It was victory, but at the cost of allowing the Antigonids back into the Peloponnese to stifle any comeback for democracy.

Over time the descendants of the Macedonian conquistadores became truly Greek. They still competed in battle, but, like

Renaissance princes, in the cultural arena too. Their cities in Egypt and Asia Minor became centers of Hellenism. From the start, the Ptolemaic rulers spared no expense in turning Alexandria into a cultural and intellectual hub to rival Athens, even going so far as to steal Alexander's body in a dramatic heist. They created the greatest library the world had ever seen, complete with museum and research zoo. On the west coast of Anatolia, Pergamum would later grow into another great center for Hellenism, its library second only to the one in Alexandria.

Alexandrian librarians were charged with collecting and cataloging the plays of Aeschylus, Sophocles, and Euripides, as well as the many versions of the Homeric epics. It is to the labors of men like Zenodotus of Ephesus and Aristophanes of Byzantion that we owe the versions of the *Iliad* and *Odyssey* that we have today.

Great Cities, Great Minds

The Hellenistic *poleis* offered similar benefits to Silicon Valley in California today. They were partially self-governing incubators of talent where good living, money, and the company of other great minds were ever-present.

Archimedes of Syracuse, Eratosthenes of Cyrene, Aristarchus of Samos, Crates of Pergamum . . . the list is endless. These men measured the world and its heavens with startling accuracy. Eratosthenes's calculation of the circumference of the planet was only a hundred miles short of the true figure of 24,901 miles. Aristarchus showed that the earth and all the other planets moved around the sun, and placed them in the correct order, some eighteen centuries before Copernicus did the same in another self-governing city, Hanseatic Kraków.

It wasn't just men. Hypatia, portrayed by Rachel Weisz in the film *Agora*, lived in the post-Hellenistic Alexandria of the fourth century CE. A brilliant philosopher, astronomer, and mathematician, she was murdered by a Christian mob for daring to resist the power-hungry Bishop Cyril.

Astrolabe, steam engine, odometer, chain drive, gimbal, water pump, central heating . . . all were invented during this time. In 1900, sponge divers near the tiny island of Antikythera came across the wreck of a Roman cargo ship filled with treasure to garnish Julius Caesar's "Triumph" through the streets of Rome. Among the loot was what became known as the Antikythera Mechanism, widely regarded as the earliest example of an analog computer. Built in the second century BCE, it has thirty-seven gear wheels and can chart the movements of the moon and sun through the zodiac. It even models the irregular orbit of the moon. Nothing of comparable complexity would appear in Europe for fourteen centuries.

The patronage of the Hellenistic kings extended to all areas of culture and science, but not to political philosophy or the search for a better way to govern. Playwrights turned away from weighty issues. The comedies of Menander (342–291 BCE) were keen observations of everyday life, full of witty and memorable aphorisms ("whom the gods love, die young") but they lack the grand ideas of an Aeschylus or the biting satire of an Aristophanes.

Greek philosophy had turned inward, and its connection with political science had been fatally severed. Hellenistic philosophers, perhaps influenced by the Hindu and Buddhist *yogin*, searched for *ataraxia* (undisturbedness), *autarky* (self-reliance), and *apatheia* (freedom from suffering). By the first decade of the third century BCE, two rival schools had emerged in Athens: Zeno of Citium's Stoicism and Epicurus of Samos's Epicureanism. Neither concerned themselves much with good government.

The purpose of philosophy was "to allay that which causes disturbance in life" (Xenocrates, head of Plato's Academy). Inner contentment, not social harmony, was the goal.

Epicureanism, Stoicism, and Christianity

Epicurus (341–270 BCE) owes his unjust reputation to the hostility of medieval Christian commentators. His ideas were rediscovered in the fifteenth century by a dogged Italian scholar named Poggio Bracciolini. In the library of a remote German monastery, Poggio came across the manuscript of *De Rerum Natura* (*On the Nature of Things*), in which the Roman philosopher Lucretius (99–55 BCE) set out Epicurus's ideas in verse. They were revolutionary: science, not the gods, makes the universe go round; happiness is freedom from the fear of those gods; all matter is made up of tiny particles in perpetual motion.

His denial of an afterlife enraged a clergy who saw terror of damnation as a useful way to control their flock, and Epicurus was ridiculed as the patron saint of slavering hedonists. Dante placed him in the Sixth Circle of Hell, where he was trapped in a flaming coffin. But far from being a hedonist, Epicurus defined pleasure as the "absence of suffering," which he believed came from a sober and moral life surrounded by friends, rather than one led in fear of eternal torment.

Stoicism was more to a churchman's liking. Its prescription for happiness lay in indifference to the pains and pleasures of the world, and in the cultivation of virtuous self-control. From here to the Christian worldview was a small step.

Philosophy's break with political science made the task of the Hellenistic rulers easier. Here was the dirty compromise at the heart of the new world order. Greek culture would be permitted to change the world, but not Greek politics.

Few cared. Civic commitment was hard work, especially if you were a hoplite. Besides, where was the enemy?

> Now what's to become of us without barbarians? These people were some sort of solution.
>
> Cavafy, Alexandrian poet (1863–1933)

The Coming of Rome

In fact, the barbarians were on their way. The Greeks had known about the Romans for a long time. There'd been Greek cities in Italy for as long as there'd been Romans, and at least one of them—*Locri Epizephyrii*—was governed by a democracy not so different from the Athenian model.

Through the third century BCE, relations between the two worsened. King Pyrrhus's invasion of Italy (280–274 BCE) lingered in Roman minds. His victories may have been proverbially pyrrhic—and he was eventually driven out—but Roman losses had been severe too. By 229 BCE, the shoe was on the other foot.

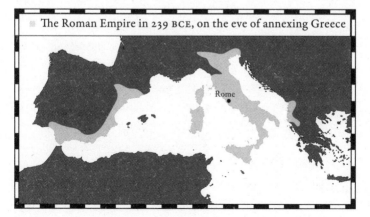

The Roman Empire in 239 BCE, on the eve of annexing Greece

For the first time, Roman armies marched onto Greek soil, ostensibly to deal with Illyrian (Albanian) pirates preying on lucrative shipping routes. But they didn't just leave, and the protectorates they left behind were their beachhead for things to come.

The Greeks didn't see what was happening until it was too late. Perhaps they hadn't realized how different the Roman *polis* was from the Greek model. Ordinary Romans were excluded from government and wielded no real power. There was no Roman version of the people's jury courts, no Pnyx. A small number of powerful families ruled Rome through the Senate, and there were few mechanisms to hold them to account. Instead of an educated, politically engaged middle class to act as a check on the elite, there was the notorious Roman mob.

Not only this, but Roman culture was defined by military success, and successful generals were given a free hand in the field. The result was a never-ending cycle of annexation. Rome's very existence depended on perpetual violence.

Between 217 and 168 BCE, the Romans pulled off a fifty-year masterstroke in which professions of friendship and shared values provided the cover for total annexation. Agelaus of the Aetolian League was one of the few to see what was coming. At a conference of Greek *poleis* near Corinth in 217 BCE, he urged the Greeks to set aside their differences and unite to face the "clouds now gathering in the west."

As Agelaus had feared, Greece was too divided to resist. On the mainland were three power blocs: Macedon in the north, the Aetolian League in the center, and the Achaean League in the Peloponnese. Over the next five decades, Rome exploited the antagonism among these three groups while seeing off the threat from Carthage. By 168 BCE, it was ready to send in the legions, and at the Battle of Pydna, thousands of Macedonians were slaughtered for the loss of only a hundred Roman soldiers. The aftermath saw some of the worst atrocities in Roman history, as Aemilius unleashed his troops to violence to discourage any thought of rebellion. They killed or enslaved 150,000 Greeks and torched the land. Even Polybius was shocked into castigating him as "the most brutal and unscrupulous monster the world has ever seen."

In the wider Hellenistic world, too, Rome's takeover was almost complete. Just outside Alexandria, the Seleucid King Antiochus was intercepted on his way to conquer the Ptolemaic lands by an elderly Roman senator, Gaius Popillius Laenas. The Senate had dispatched him to deliver a simple message: "Turn back." Antiochus asked for time to talk things over with his advisers, but Laenas drew a circle around him in the sand and insisted that he receive an answer before Antiochus breached its perimeter. With his whole army behind him and a single Roman senator before him, Antiochus did indeed turn back. It was clear that there was now only one superpower in the Mediterranean world.

In 146 BCE, with Carthage finally defeated, the Romans were ready to finish the job in Greece. The Achaean League, having been provoked into rebellion, was annihilated in battle. The city of Corinth was razed to the ground, its male population killed and its women and children sold into slavery.

> The Romans created a wilderness and called it peace.
>
> Tacitus

Rebellion and Retribution

Direct rule from Rome was a rude shock to the *poleis* of Greece and Asia, which found themselves heinously overtaxed by the voracious late Republic. One last great convulsion of Greek independence was the result.

In 88 BCE, Mithridates VI of Pontus called on the people of Asia Minor to rise up and massacre their Roman neighbors. The suffering Greeks heeded his call: eighty thousand Roman settlers were murdered across Greece and Anatolia. The Roman general Manius Aquillius, caught on Lesbos as he tried to escape, had molten gold poured down his throat.

His part-Persian ancestry notwithstanding, Mithridates presented himself as the champion of the Greeks and persuaded the cities of the mainland, including Athens, to defect to his cause. Retribution was swift and terrible. Rome's greatest general, Sulla, landed in Illyria and marched straight to Athens. After a five-month siege in which the citizens were reduced to eating shoe leather and grass, Athens was taken in a midnight attack. Contemporaries claimed that its streets literally ran with blood.

Intriguingly, even in the midst of the siege, Athenians seem to have retained an unshakable sense of their own superiority. A delegation came out of the city to treat Sulla to a lecture on the glory of Athens, prompting a curt response:

I was sent to Athens not to take lessons but to reduce rebels to obedience.

It would take three wars fought by Rome's finest generals over twenty-five years to defeat Mithridates and recover Asia Minor. Never again would the Greeks seriously consider revolt, turning their talents instead to the more promising business of making their conquerors more Greek. Yet even among the Greeks, there were some who fervently admired the Roman way.

Polybius and the Roman Way

The Romans learned early the benefits of bringing their enemies to Rome to educate them. Nowhere is this better illustrated than in the case of Polybius. Born around 210 BCE into one of the leading families of the Achaean League, he was among the thousand hostages sent to Rome in 167 BCE. He stayed for seventeen years, mixing with the grandest Roman families (including that of the "monster" Aemilius) and becoming thoroughly indoctrinated in the Roman way of life and government.

When Aemilius's son, Scipio Aemilianus, sacked Carthage in 146 BCE, Polybius was there. When Corinth was sacked later that year, he was there too. He witnessed the brutality of his hosts firsthand, yet he was dazzled by their success. Above all, he was fascinated by how the Republic had managed to recover from the disaster of Cannae in 216 BCE—when an entire army had been wiped out by the Carthaginian general, Hannibal—to rule the world just fifty years later. This was to become the subject of his *Histories*.

Polybius was no democrat. He agreed with Aristotle that "extreme democracy" led to mob rule (or *ochlocracy*—a term he coined, *ochlos* meaning "mob"), but rejected the philosopher's *polity*. He thought the Greek *polis* was trapped in a perpetual cycle of tyranny-democracy-ochlocracy, or what he called *anacyclosis*.

According to Polybius, the Romans had managed to break free of this cycle via a constitution that perfectly balanced monarchical, aristocratic, and plebeian power: the "best political order yet realized among men." This matters because it was to Polybius rather than to Greek political thinkers that the Founding Fathers looked when writing the American Constitution of 1787. This landowning, slaveholding elite did not want true civic participation to interrupt the happy business of creating more wealth for themselves. "How is it we hear the loudest yelps for liberty among the drivers of negroes?" asked

Samuel Johnson in 1775. America's founders might call what they were creating a democracy, but it was deliberately very different from the *demokratia* of ancient Athens.

The representative system of government that exists today across the West has more to do with Rome than Athens and, to its cost, very little indeed to do with civic involvement.

Difficult Embrace

The Greek historian Dionysius of Halicarnassus argued that since Rome was fundamentally a Greek city, Greeks should not despise Romans. But despise them they did. One problem was the Roman addiction to violence. The Greeks did not flock to watch mass slaughter. Even their plays tended to have violence described by the messenger rather than enacted on stage (the famous exception being Euripides's *Bacchae*, first performed just before the end of the Peloponnesian War). Greece had citizens. Rome had a bestial mob that had to be kept docile with bread and circuses.

Roman attitudes to the Greeks blended the insecurity and scorn often felt by nouveaux riches toward something older, particularly when it's the source of those *riches*. Rome owed its wealth to war booty, including slaves, and to the extortionate taxation of conquered peoples. So much Greek money poured into the Roman treasury after Pydna that domestic land taxation was canceled indefinitely. Small wonder the Greeks had flocked to Mithridates and his calls for violent rebellion.

In a famous letter to his son, the Roman historian and senator Cato (234–149 BCE) characterizes the Greeks as a "worthless and unruly race," urging him never to consult a Greek doctor "for they have sworn to kill all barbarians." For Cato, the plunder from Greece and Asia Minor was driving obscene extremes of wealth, and laying waste to "honest" Roman values.

Few were listening. Rome was the most glorious empire the world had ever seen, and its first emperor, Augustus, was spending the plunder on creating a capital worthy of it. "I found Rome a city of bricks and left it a city of marble," he boasted.

In 27 BCE Greece was formally annexed into the Roman Empire as the Province of Achaea.

THE GRECO-ROMAN EMPIRE (168 BCE–330 CE)

> Captive Greece captured her rude conqueror.
>
> Horace (65–8 BCE), Roman poet

In 117 CE the Roman Empire was at its height, home to sixty million people (about a quarter of the world's population) and ruled by Hadrian, a passionate Hellenophile. His statue at the Nymphaion in Olympia speaks volumes. He wears a breastplate emblazoned with the image of the goddess Athena standing over the she-wolf that suckles the twin founders of Rome. This was an empire that knew how much it owed to the Greeks.

It might have been even more Greek. If Mark Antony and his wife, Cleopatra, had defeated Octavian (later Augustus) at the Battle of Actium in 31 BCE, Alexandria could well have become the Imperial HQ, with Rome a mere provincial capital.

As it was, the empire had Greek gods, Greek forms of government (albeit not very democratic ones), Greek art, and a largely Greek-manned civil service. The long history of the Greeks was central to Rome's idea of itself. The Homeric Age had given Rome its gods and the basis for its own founding myth, the *Aeneid*—a Latin version of the *Odyssey* presented by Virgil to Augustus in 19 BCE. Horace, born five years after Virgil, was educated in Athens and modeled his *Odes* on early Greek lyric poets such as Pindar and Sappho. Not much later, Ovid would retell the Greek myths in his *Metamorphoses*.

What of the *polis*? Like the Hellenistic version, the Roman *polis* had most of the outward characteristics of its Greek ancestor (agora, theater, baths) but it lacked its political life. Some "free cities" had a measure of independence, but in the end all were subject to the emperor. Hadrian, in love with all things Greek— including the beautiful youth Antinous, whose statue he erected all over the empire—tried to restore some of Greece's classical past with the Athens-led Panhellenium League, but it never really got off the ground.

Nevertheless, Athens was the nerve center of intellectual life in the Roman Empire, educating not only poets like Horace but emperors from Nero to Marcus Aurelius. Until the coming of Christianity, most Roman philosophy centered around two Greek traditions: the Epicurean (Lucretius), and Stoic (Seneca, Marcus Aurelius).

Greek artists versed in the classical tradition traveled en masse to Italy, where the Roman elite filled their palaces and gardens with copies of statues by Phidias and Praxiteles. It was Greek architects and sculptors who helped Augustus build his "city of marble" with ideas and material plundered from their homeland. Perhaps it isn't surprising that the Greek heart wasn't in it. "Art stopped then," according to Pliny the Elder (23–79 CE). There would be no Roman equivalent to the Parthenon marbles.

If Athens provided one kind of entertainment, Sparta offered another. Granted special free-city status as a reward for the military support it had given Octavian-Augustus against Mark Antony, it seems to have turned itself into a kind of war-themed Disneyland, popular with monied Roman tourists in search of an exotic break.

At the crossroads of trade between Rome and the East, the Greek mainland prospered. Corinth, rebuilt by Julius Caesar in 46 BCE as the new capital of Achaia, grew rapidly. By the third century CE, it controlled overland trade in and out of the Peloponnese and boasted a temple to Aphrodite that employed some thousand temple prostitutes. Pleasure didn't come cheap. As Horace commented (laconically): "Not everyone can go to Corinth."

The Greek archipelago flourished too. For centuries the tiny island of Delos, as the birthplace of the twin gods Apollo and Artemis, had been a sacred and pristine site of pilgrimage. Now the Romans turned the barren island into one of the busiest, wealthiest, and most cosmopolitan commercial hubs in the world. Today you can see the ruins of its Syrian and Egyptian temples alongside huge theaters, agoras, and two-story villas floored with exquisite mosaics.

Yet Greece, though it was rich and influential, was not what it had been. Perhaps nowhere was this better displayed than at the Olympic Games. In 67 CE, in the early years of the empire, Nero decided to compete. He won every event he took part in, including a ten-horse chariot race in which he'd actually been ejected from his chariot. The Games would limp on for three centuries or so until, with the barbarians at the gate, the Emperor Theodosius finally abolished them.

THE GREEK EMPIRE (330–1460 CE)

If you lined up the world's great empires in order of longevity, Britain's would be near the back. Somewhere between three and six centuries is the average, with a few more recent examples, such as Germany's Third Reich, not even managing a decade. Only one survived more than a millennium, for most of which it was the leading military and economic force of its continent.

This was the Greek Empire. It spanned the 1,130 years from the foundation of Constantinople in 330 to the final surrender of the Peloponnese to the Ottomans in 1460. It was the Victorians who named the empire Byzantium, recognizing that although the people had called themselves *Rhomaioi*, they were very different from their contemporaries in Rome. Culturally, linguistically, and for the most part ethnically, they were Greek.

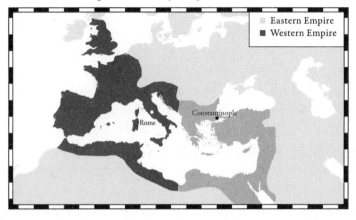

Ever since the conquest of Greece and the eastern Hellenistic kingdoms, Rome had comprised two distinct halves: a backward, Latin-speaking West and a more urban, advanced, Greek-speaking East. In 285, Emperor Diocletian formalized things by splitting the empire in two, taking the *pars orientalis* for himself and giving the West to his co-emperor, Maximilian. By the time Constantine I (272–337) made himself sole emperor again, the main threat was from the Sassanids in today's Iran. The East was the source of the wealth that kept the legions in the field, and Rome needed a new capital to reflect its new priorities.

Constantine's eye fell upon Byzantion, a small, maritime Greek city founded a thousand years before. It occupied a nearly impregnable position on the threshold of Asia, just where East met West.

On Monday, May 11, 330, the emperor formally dedicated his new city to the Virgin Mary, and Constantinople was born.

How can we explain the longevity of this new Greek Empire? Wealth is part of the answer: the riches of the East funded large, well-equipped armies. Christian piety also played a role as a binding agent, thickening over the centuries until, on the eve of destruction in 1453, the people of Constantinople firmly expected that the Virgin would appear to save "Her" city. Where secular philosophical ideals had once inspired citizens, now it was the Word. But the new religion had little to do with Homeric or Aristotelian human empowerment. It exhorted people to endure their suffering, not to root out its cause. And to the relief of tax collectors everywhere, it urged believers to "give unto Caesar what is Caesar's." Could any shred of *demokratia* left over from Roman times survive such a Word?

The Empire Goes Greek

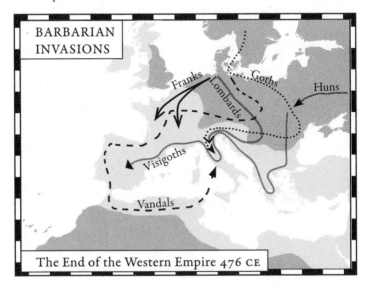

THE BARBARIAN INVASIONS

The End of the Western Empire 476 CE

The first three hundred years were still Greco-*Roman*. Theodosius I (379–395) ruled both halves of the empire, though they did not always work together. In the late fourth century, as the West succumbed to barbarians, the East used its considerable financial resources to bribe them to stay away. When bribery didn't work, the Greeks assimilated the invaders instead: after Alaric the Visigoth sacked southern Greece, the eastern Emperor Arcadius made him a general.

The eastern empire also spent money building up its defenses. At their core were the magnificent triple walls of Constantinople, which would protect the city for the next eight hundred years. Constantinople seemed invulnerable, and its citizens began to call it *Basileuousa*, the "Queen of Cities."

The last emperor to speak Latin before Greek was Justinian I (482–565). From humble roots himself, he married Theodora, a performer with the grit of the circus beneath her fingernails. When the Constantinople mob threatened to unseat him in the Nika Riots, it was she who persuaded Justinian to face them down rather than flee. Almost as tough was Justinian's brilliant general, Belisarius, who led the campaign to recapture the western empire. It was under Justinian that the empire's laws were first codified, and the Code of Justinian still forms the basis of Greek law today.

The Nika Riots

One unwelcome Roman inheritance the new Greek Empire couldn't shake off was the mob. It's a sign of how times had changed since the Athenian Golden Age that contemporary writers used the word *demokratia* to describe its riots.

In the old days, the mob had been pacified with bread and circuses. By the time of Justinian, its violent energies were being channeled through competitive sport in the hippodrome.

Before the chariot races began, the emperor would allow the crowd to voice its objection to, for instance, high prices, by means of ritualized chanting.

Sometimes ritual wasn't enough. In 532, the crowd broke out of the hippodrome and began to attack the palace next door. Over the next five days, half of Constantinople was burned to the ground, including Justinian's new Church of the Hagia Sophia. Finally, at Theodora's urging, Justinian sent in the troops. Led by Belisarius, they slaughtered over thirty thousand of the rebels. No rebellion on this scale was ever to break out again.

Justinian's rebuilding of Constantinople had been expensive, which may be why his successor failed to pay the Persians the usual tribute. The Sassanian invasion that followed proved an invitation to opportunists everywhere. The Lombards seized the moment to invade Italy, while the Avars and Slavs moved on the Balkans. Suddenly the empire was assaulted from all sides. The Sassanids pushed deep into the Levant, taking Damascus and Jerusalem, then crossed Anatolia to join the Avars and Slavs in besieging Constantinople.

Cometh the hour. Heraclius was the son of one of the empire's African governors. He sailed from Egypt to Constantinople, overthrew the unpopular Emperor Phocas, and took the throne himself. Then he rebuilt the army, lifted the siege, and drove the Persians deep into their own territory, defeating them at Nineveh in 627. He went on to take their capital, Ctesiphon, near today's Baghdad, and even recovered the True Cross, the most holy relic in Christendom.

Heraclius's capture of the True Cross and its return to Jerusalem confirmed his belief in divine intervention. Indeed, his counterattack against the Persians was waged as a kind of crusade, with the image of Christ carried ahead of the army. All this deepened still further the relationship between the emperor and his powerful patriarch, Sergius, who'd supported every inch of his campaign, even melting down Church treasures to replenish the imperial coffers.

Emperor and Patriarch

The partnership between emperor and patriarch was at the center of the Byzantine world. When the two met at the vast doors of Hagia Sophia (reserved for their use only) and processed together down the aisle, the intended message was that Church and State were joined at the hip, mutually basking in the blessing of the Almighty.

Yet the symbolic equality was deceptive. From the start, Constantine had placed the Church firmly under his thumb, personally presiding over the councils that decided doctrine and liturgy. The eastern patriarchs would never wield the power-broking clout of the western popes, but then the East was not teeming with rival princes with whom a canny pontiff could play divide-and-rule.

Heraclius adopted the Greek title *Basileus* rather than Roman *Imperator*, replaced Latin with Greek as the official tongue, and changed the currency from the Roman *solidus* to the Greek *nomisma*. All this expressed a clear intent to change the empire into something more Greek.

A New God

In 632, as Muhammad was exhaling his final breath in the desert town of Medina, the empire was under huge strain. Despite Heraclius's military successes, it was practically broke, and it was still reeling from the "Plague of Justinian" that had killed half of Europe. It was completely unprepared for the tornado that would roar out of the Arabian peninsula and in just fifty years brush aside the Sassanid Empire to hammer at the gates of Constantinople.

The jihad launched by Muhammad's heirs had no less an ambition than world dominion. The Arab armies adopted a vast pincer movement to encircle Europe. One crossed north Africa before heading up through Spain and reaching within two hundred miles of Paris. The other, larger by far, overran the empire's richest provinces of Egypt and Syria before racing across Anatolia to lay siege to Constantinople itself.

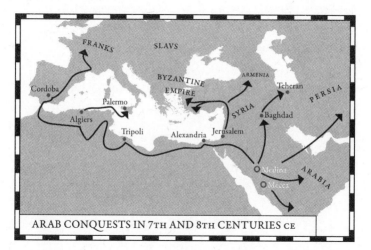

ARAB CONQUESTS IN 7TH AND 8TH CENTURIES CE

In two great sieges (674–678 and 717–718) the Arabs threw everything they had at Constantinople's massive walls. They were defeated by those walls, as well as by weather, disease, and the wonder-weapon of "Greek fire." Another product of Hellenistic inventiveness, this was a secret mix of naphtha and quicklime, which ignited on contact with water. With its fleet burned to cinders, the Muslim army turned back. Europe was saved, and thanks, as always, went to God.

Byzantine Piety: Icons and Iconoclasm

Icons may have their roots in the *fayyum* funerary portraits of late Hellenistic Egypt. With their blend of precision and mystical power, they were extraordinarily popular in the Byzantine Empire.

But after the first onslaught of Islam, people in the eastern provinces began to wonder if the Arabs owed their success to their avoidance of graven images (for which, after all, there was plenty of support in the Bible). Over the next century or so, icons were smashed, frescoes scrubbed away, and heads torn off statues. Some saw the battles won during this period against Arabs, Slavs, and Bulgars as proof that this iconoclastic frenzy had regained God's favor.

But Greeks in the West had never supported iconoclasm, and eventually they prevailed. It was two empresses, Irene and Theodora, who were responsible for reversing the policy.

Egyptian funerary portrait (pre-250 CE) and Byzantine icon (590–600 CE)

A New Golden Age

The Arab invaders hadn't captured the Queen of Cities, but the empire's territory had shrunk by two thirds (only the Greek mainland, the Balkans, and Anatolia remained) and its income by three quarters. Leo III and his son, Constantine V, reorganized what was left into *themata*. It was a practical solution, enabled by an administrative system that had somehow survived the storm. Each *thema* was defended by an army of farmer-soldier-citizens living on state-leased land—they were almost hoplites—under the command of a *strategos*, or general. The most vulnerable frontier districts were further broken down into *kleisourai*, tasked with repulsing guerrilla raids.

The *themata* worked well both in a military and a fiscal sense. By 850 the empire had recovered much of Anatolia, and its income had doubled, an extraordinary achievement given that it had lost the wealth of Syria, the Levant, and Egypt.

It was the dawn of a new golden age. The resurgent Byzantium was strikingly meritocratic: men of talent, whatever their origins, could rise to the top. Birth still mattered but the vast imperial administration made for a solid middle class, one of Aristotle's prerequisites for a well-run state. Another—education, or *paideia*—was similarly promoted, and the curriculum hadn't much changed since the philosopher's day. It was still based on the seven liberal arts: grammar, logic, rhetoric, arithmetic, geometry, harmonics, and astronomy, with Greek philosophical argument underpinning it all. Educated citizens knew by heart the poetry of Homer, the fables of Aesop, the plays of Aeschylus, and the speeches of Demosthenes. The more recent Christian learning was a complement, not an alternative.

The careers of the emperors themselves inspired social mobility, however violently they'd ascended the throne. Justinian I

(482–565) was born a peasant, as was Michael II (770–829), founder of the Amorian dynasty. Both had risen through the ranks of the army. In the first half of the ninth century, another peasant rose to the imperial diadem, this time through the court: Basil I (811–886), founder of the Macedonian dynasty.

The Bride Show

The bride show was certainly the most dramatic example of Byzantine social mobility, if not exactly of meritocracy. From the eighth century or perhaps even earlier, some emperors selected their wives by means of a beauty contest in which the empire's most desirable maidens were paraded for his—and no doubt his mother's—inspection. Everyone was eligible, however lowly her origins. Leo IV (750–780) seems to have chosen Irene of Athens in this way, and Theodora certainly married Theophilos via the bride show in 829. This union was providential. After her husband died, Theodora presided over a regency that not only extinguished the last embers of iconoclasm, but also persuaded the Bulgars not to invade. There is no evidence that the bride shows continued after the eleventh century, but that didn't stop a much later generation of Victorian painters from fantasizing extensively on the theme.

Assimilating the Barbarians

Under the Macedonian dynasty (867–1056), the empire reached its peak of post-Muhammad wealth, territory, and cultural brilliance. Basil I stabilized the frontiers and replenished the coffers, then his successors took back much of the lost eastern territory. In the West, though, the Bulgars were resurgent. The hour once again called for an exceptional leader—and that this emperor is known to posterity as "Basil the Bulgar-Slayer" (reigned 976–1025) suggests he met with some success. By 1018, the Danube frontier, not held since the seventh century, had been restored and Bulgaria was part of the empire.

Despite his fearsome moniker, Basil seems to fit surprisingly well Aristotle's definition of the enlightened monarch:

> We have observed with our own eyes . . . the avarice and injustice every day perpetrated against the poor. The powerful who desire to aggrandize and to enjoy in full ownership what they had wrongly expropriated at the expense of the law . . . will be stripped of the property belonging to others.
>
> Preamble to a law of 996

He didn't just slay barbarians; he assimilated them too. It was during Basil's reign that the historic bond between Greece and Russia was forged. Vladimir the Great (958–1015) converted to Christianity in 988 and Kievan Rus joined the Orthodox community of nations. Religious partnership broadened into mutual trade, cultural exchange, and dynastic intermarriage. Vladimir even gifted Basil the Varangian Guard, a regiment of terrifying Nordic giants with double-headed axes who became the imperial bodyguard.

Twelfth-century depiction of the Varangian Guard, with Viking weaponry

In assimilating their neighbors, the Byzantine Greeks were following the ancient custom of *xenia*, or "hospitality," one of the wellsprings of Greek identity and history. From the seventh century onward, the chief response of the Greeks to Slavic infiltration of the Balkans was not to drive the incomers away, but to draw them into their own social and commercial networks. Over time, many Slavs became Christian, Greek-speaking, tax-paying subjects of the emperor.

Cyril and Methodius: "Apostles to the Slavs"

The Orthodox religion was a powerful force for assimilation. In the ninth century, Patriarch Photios commissioned two Greek brothers from Thessaloniki to come up with a way of writing down the Slavonic language. Cyril had been professor of philosophy at Constantinople, and Methodius the abbot of a monastery. The outcome was the Cyrillic alphabet, which would take the Gospel not just to the Slavs of the Balkans, but to Russia.

It caused outrage in the West. At a famous debate held in Venice in 867, western bishops attacked Cyril and Methodius "like ravens against a falcon" for taking the liturgy beyond the three sacred languages of Hebrew, Greek, and Latin. Cyril's eloquent defense prefigures the words of later reformers like Martin Luther: "Falls not God's rain upon all equally? And shines not the sun upon all?"

By Basil's death in 1025, the Greek imperium stretched from southern Italy to Armenia, and its revenues were almost at pre-Arab conquest levels. Once again it was indisputably the richest, most powerful force in Christendom, and Constantinople was by far Europe's greatest city.

BYZANTINE EMPIRE c. 1025

But for all his talents, the Bulgar-Slayer had produced no heir, and after his death the empire fell under the leadership of lesser men. The army was neglected and the currency debased. New enemies appeared on the borders: the Normans in Italy, the Seljuk Turks in the east. At the Battle of Manzikert in 1071, the Greek army was catastrophically defeated by the Turks, and the emperor himself taken prisoner. Within a decade, the Seljuks had taken over nearly all of Anatolia and founded their capital in Nicaea, just sixty miles east of Constantinople.

The Empire Strikes Back

Emperor Alexios ascended the throne in 1081. During his thirty-seven-year rule, he took back much of Anatolia, rid Thessaly of the Normans, and Thrace of the Central Asian Pechenegs. He also tamed the troublesome imperial elite, creating a new power network based on kinship. His family and their descendants would preside over the various parts of the empire for the next 350 years.

Perhaps Alexios's biggest success was to restore the currency. During the seven centuries from 312, when Constantine had issued the first *solidus*, to 1021, when Basil II issued the last, the

Greek currency had been extraordinarily stable, backed by a reliable system of tax collection and Constantinople's status as the world's greatest trading city. Its coinage underpinned international trade in much the same way as the dollar does today. But from 1021 frequent devaluations had stoked inflation. In 1092, Alexios introduced the new *hyperpyron*, restoring much of the gold content to the coinage.

East-West Relations

With the crowning of Charlemagne in 800, much of what had been the western Roman Empire was again united under one leader. For the first time, its peoples identified themselves as Europeans—and Europe meant above all Christendom. The Byzantine Greek Empire was Christian too—indeed had twice saved its brothers in God from the swords of Islam—but there was a growing sense of religious and cultural incompatibility between East and West. Charlemagne's assumption of the title Holy Roman Emperor didn't help. Where did that leave the emperor in Constantinople?

As Europe grew in wealth and confidence over the next two centuries, with the great trading cities of Venice and Genoa leading the way, "Greek" became a derogatory term expressing both religious and social aversion. Things came to a head in 1054, when pope and patriarch mutually excommunicated each other, opening a schism between the Catholic and Orthodox Churches that still exists today.

The Crusades

It was hardly an auspicious time to ask for help, but in 1095 Alexios was forced to request mercenaries from the pope to help fight the Turks. The response was more than he had bargained for. On November 27, Pope Urban II rose to his feet at the Council of Clermont in France and called for a "crusade" to win back the Holy Land.

> Your brethren who live in the east are in urgent need of your help. . . . [It is time] to carry aid to those Christians and to destroy that vile race from the lands of our friends.

Before long, an army of crusaders was camped outside Constantinople on its way to do just that. Alexios summoned their leaders and made them swear an oath that all land and cities recovered en route would be given back to the empire.

If the crusaders ever intended to honor their promise, they'd changed their minds by the time they captured Antioch. It isn't hard to see why. At Constantinople, the knights of the First Crusade would have experienced both dazzling wealth and agonizing condescension. To their hosts, such as the emperor's daughter Anna, they seemed a smelly, boorish, illiterate rabble. In her account of their arrival at Constantinople, she refused even to mention them by name, citing her "inability to make unpronounceable barbaric sounds."*

As the crusaders ravaged their way through Anatolia, they began to hear rumors of Greek parley with the Turk. So once they'd taken Antioch, they wondered why they should return the prize to the cowardly, schismatic snobs whose war they were winning for them. Instead, they made the city capital of one of four new Crusader States in the Levant.

In the end the First Crusade did recover much of the Anatolian plateau for the empire, and Alexios's successors continued to push back the frontiers. But a whole new level of mutual mistrust had entered the relationship.

---

* The quote comes from the *Alexiad*, an epic account of Alexios's reign written by his adoring daughter Anna, who had an eye for, if not an obsession with, the niceties of class.

> Ever since our rough crusading forefathers first saw Constantinople and met, to their contemptuous disgust, a society where everyone read and wrote, ate food with forks and preferred diplomacy to war, it has been fashionable to pass the Byzantines by with scorn and to use their name as synonymous with decadence.
>
> Steven Runciman, *The Emperor Romanus Lecapenus and His Reign: A Study of Tenth-Century Byzantium*, 1988

Byzantine Law

It was the Romans who brought written law to the eastern Mediterranean, but the Byzantines built on their foundation. Theodosius II (401–450) and Justinian (482–565 CE) produced their own legal codes and established state-funded law schools. In 726, Leo III issued his *Ecloga*, which among other things bolstered the rights of wives and children. In 1047, Constantine IX opened a school of law and a school of philosophy in Constantinople. The latter was under the direction of Michael Psellos, a brilliant polymath, though tellingly Latin was not his strength: he is said to have muddled Cicero and Caesar.

Aristotle thought a ruler should not only be bound by the law, but be its chief living practitioner. On Fridays, accompanied by various high officials, the emperor would process from the Great Palace to the Church of Blachernai. Along the way, citizens were free to present appeals to him in person. On one occasion, Emperor Theophilos (805–42) was petitioned by a widow who claimed that the horse on which a member of his entourage rode belonged to her. Theophilos had the matter investigated on the spot, found in favor of the widow, and returned her horse. The official turned up to Mass on foot.

For the time being, though, there was peace, and with it economic growth. In the first decades of the twelfth century, the empire's population surged, cities were made over, and trade networks opened up to the new Crusader Kingdoms. There was a cultural renaissance too, and a new enthusiasm for classical learning, which had been in decline since the seventh century. It was at this time that the first major transfer of ancient Greek texts to the West began. Classical Greek science, philosophy, and mathematics, alongside the crucial advances of medieval Arabic scholars, could now be studied in the new universities of Bologna, Salamanca, and Paris. Literary and historical texts would follow.

Massacre of the Latins

Slowly but surely, though, the geopolitical tectonic plates were shifting. The Venetians and Genoese were making ever-deeper inroads into the empire's trade network, and they began to flex their muscles. In return for ferrying imperial troops—the empire's navy having been decimated by cuts—the Venetians demanded trading privileges that put Byzantine merchants at a disadvantage. When John II failed to renew those privileges after Alexios's death, the Venetians simply raided the Greek islands until he did.

In April 1182, an imperial pretender named Andronikos whipped up the anti-Latin sentiment of the mob to clear his way to the throne. Decades of pent-up religious, cultural, and commercial resentment against crusaders, Italian merchants—against the West in general—exploded into violence. In the Massacre of the Latins, most of the city's sixty-thousand-strong Roman Catholic community, including women, children, and the elderly, were slaughtered, enslaved, or forced to flee for their lives.

The Rape of the Queen

Nineteen years later when the leaders of the imminent Fourth Crusade assembled in Venice, that massacre must have been fresh in their minds. They were there to commission ships to ferry an army of thirty-five thousand crusaders across the Mediterranean to conquer Egypt, the most powerful Muslim state of the day. Their plan was to move north from there to retake Jerusalem, lost in 1187 to the Kurdish warrior Saladin.

It turned out that they had overestimated the crusading zeal of their populations. Only a third of the expected number of soldiers gathered in Venice the following year. In lieu of payment for the ships not now needed, the Venetians demanded that the crusaders take back the city of Zara from their regional rivals, the Croato-Hungarians. Zara was duly besieged—despite the Pope's threat to excommunicate all who took part in the Catholic-on-Catholic attack—and returned to Venice.

The crusaders were then paid a visit by Prince Alexios, son of Emperor Isaac II, who had recently been ousted in a coup. Alexios offered the irresistibly vast reward of 200,000 marks if they diverted to Constantinople and restored his father (still imprisoned in the city, having been blinded by the usurpers) to the throne. After a few weeks of siege in the summer of 1203, Isaac was back in the imperial purple, with Alexios installed as co-emperor.

Now, though, camped outside the city's walls, the crusaders learned that the emperor couldn't pay up. With the blind, octogenarian Doge Dandolo of Venice at their head, they did the impossible. They took Constantinople.

So began the rape of the Queen of Cities. A thousand years of priceless culture was looted and taken west, most of it to Venice. Catholic Christian slaughtered Orthodox Christian, as

A 15th-century depiction of the 1204 Sack of Constantinople

the antagonism of centuries was unleashed in an orgy of violence. "There was never a greater crime against humanity," wrote the historian Steven Runciman. Some eight hundred years later, the Papacy would issue an apology of sorts:

> Some memories are especially painful, and some events of the distant past have left deep wounds in the minds and hearts of people to this day. I am thinking of the disastrous sack of the imperial city of Constantinople, which was for so long the bastion of Christianity in the East. It is tragic that the assailants, who had set out to secure free access for Christians to the Holy Land, turned against their own brothers in the faith. The fact that they were Latin Christians fills Catholics with deep regret. How can we fail to see here the *mysterium iniquitatis* at work in the human heart?
>
> Pope John Paul II, 2001

Horses, Snakes, and a Hideous Lion

Among the treasures carried off to Venice were the four bronze horses of the Hippodrome, copies of which now stride over the façade of St. Mark's basilica. They could have met a worse fate. The huge statue of Hercules by Lysippos, Alexander the Great's court sculptor, was melted down by the crusaders for bronze, and the golden bowl atop the Hippodrome's Serpentine Column—which itself had been looted by Constantine from Delphi—was destroyed or stolen.

Not every work had a happy exile in Venice. Outside the arsenal is a sixth-century BCE lion that once roared a silent welcome to the sun as it rose every morning over the sacred island of Delos. It was shipped to Venice by the doge at the end of the seventeenth century but lost its head during the journey. Undismayed, the Venetians simply stuck on a hideous new one of their own making.

The Final Rally

Not many Crusaders actually went on to Jerusalem. Most stayed put in Constantinople. This occupation is known as the Latin Empire, and though it only lasted fifty-seven years (1204–1261), it delivered a mortal wound. The city's population dwindled rapidly, and farms grew up on abandoned land inside its walls. Yet the Greeks would manage one last comeback, and once again it would prove vital for the future of Europe.

With Constantinople gone, the rest of the empire splintered into three smaller versions of itself. Greek bureaucracy showed its resilience, as the cities of Nicaea, Trebizond, and Arta became the capitals of three, vibrant mini-empires. The largest was Nicaea (today's Iznik), ruled by the Laskaris family, and it was they who in 1261 took advantage of an absent Latin army to regain Constantinople.

But it was the Palaiologos dynasty, whose founder Michael VIII ousted the Laskaris, that presided over the final two hundred years of the Greek Empire. This was a time of shrinking resources and nonstop disasters, both natural and man-made. Plague after plague struck: Constantinople was the Black Death's first European port of call in 1347, when it ravaged the population, killing one of the emperor's sons.

Meanwhile, the Bulgarians and Serbs closed in from the west, and the Ottoman Turks raided further and further into Anatolia. When an earthquake destroyed most of Gallipoli and forced the inhabitants to flee in March 1354, the Turks seized the opportunity. For the first time, they crossed into Europe, claiming the abandoned territory.

Plague

The ancient Greeks knew about plague. The very first chapter of the *Iliad* tells of a plague sent by Apollo to punish the Greeks for abducting the daughter of his high priest.

The Athenian plague of 430 BCE, in the second year of the Peloponnesian War, wiped out a third of the city's population and contributed to the city's defeat by Sparta.

Since then, two bubonic plagues caused by the bacterium *Yersinia pestis* have come to Europe via Constantinople. The first struck in 541 CE during the reign of Justinian. It arrived via fleas carried by rats on a grain ship from Egypt, and at its height it was killing ten thousand citizens of Constantinople every day. Over the next two centuries it came and went, helping to weaken the empire's ability to resist the Arab invasions.

The second, the Black Death, was brought to Constantinople in 1347 by Genoese merchants fleeing the Mongols. The story goes that the Mongol army, struck down with the disease while besieging the Genoese colony of Caffa in the Crimea, catapulted their dead over the walls, in what may be the first example of biological warfare. The infected merchants took to their ships and sailed first to Constantinople, then Genoa and Venice. A year later, the plague would enter England through the port of Weymouth.

By 1380, the empire was down to just Constantinople and its hinterland, and the Peloponnese. It had no money—even the crown jewels had been pawned to Venice—no army, and no navy. Yet it managed to survive another eighty years. How?

The Greeks had one skill left in their armory, born with the Olympic Games and honed over two millennia: the subtle art of diplomacy. As Greek chariots had replaced Roman gladiators in the arena, so the guiding spirit of the empire moved from war to war by other means.

Greek Diplomacy

Since many and various matters lead toward one end, victory, it is a matter of indifference which one uses to reach it.

John Kinnamos, Imperial Secretary

Diplomacy meant understanding your neighbors. The Bureau of Barbarians was set up in Constantinople in the fifth century. Its purpose was to know everything about friend and foe alike. It was the first foreign intelligence agency, and one of its favorite tricks was to bring the sons of foreign rulers to Constantinople so that they could be educated (or reeducated).

The Byzantines used their ancient heritage to impress and influence their neighbors. Deluxe editions of classical works were presented to foreign rulers as they passed through. Copies were dispatched to the Abbasid Caliphate in Baghdad for its House of Wisdom, an institution not unlike the library of Alexandria. People were sent, too. Theophilos of Edessa, for example, served as court astrologer to the Caliph Al-Mahdi.

The diplomatic ace in the pack was the emperor himself, and the Greeks used all their ingenuity to make him seem as awesome as possible. Visitors would walk past rows of gigantic Varangian guards before reaching a throne room where mechanical lions roared and golden birds sang from golden trees. The emperor seemed to levitate before them, the result of some unseen wizardry. The tenth-century envoy Liutprand of Cremona was quite dazzled: "Behold! The man whom just before I had seen sitting on a moderately elevated seat had now changed his raiment and was sitting on the level of the ceiling."

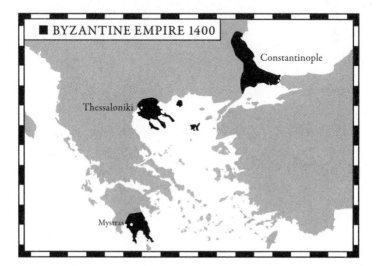

BYZANTINE EMPIRE 1400

Constantinople

Thessaloniki

Mystras

By the start of the fifteenth century, Constantinople was under more or less permanent siege by the Ottoman Sultan, Bayezid. Manuel II's humiliating cap-in-hand tour of European courts came to nothing. In 1401, he even tried to tap England, spending Christmas with King Henry IV at Eltham Palace. A grand joust was held in his honor, but there was no gold under the tree on Christmas morning.

It was from the East that temporary salvation came. Tamerlaine, a new Mongol warlord sucked from the very depths of hell, had already slaughtered some nineteen million human beings in carving out his vast Asian empire. Now it was rubbing up against Bayezid's Ottoman territory. Tensions rose, as the tyrants exchanged ever more baroque insults:

> Since the ship of your unfathomable ambition has been shipwrecked in the abyss of self-love, it would be wise for you to lower the sails of your rashness and cast the anchor of repentance in the port of sincerity, which is also the port of safety; lest, by the tempest of our vengeance you should perish in the sea of punishment which you deserve.
>
> Letter from Tamerlaine to Bayezid

The Battle of Ankara in 1402 was one of the most vital in European history. Tamerlaine destroyed Bayezid's army, capturing the sultan himself and granting Europe time to prepare for the Ottoman assault to come.*

Why did he do it? Tamerlaine's burning ambition had always been to conquer China, as his forebears had done. He'd been planning it for years. It's tempting to imagine Byzantine diplomats

---

* Legend has it that Tamerlaine kept Bayezid in a cage as a kind of pet until he died of shame.

expertly goading him into seeking vengeance on Bayezid. Their influence might even explain why the Mongol army did not press on after the victory at Ankara to take Constantinople.

The Battle of Ankara made possible another half-century of imperial life. It wasn't much of a life, though. The patient was suffering organ collapse and could barely function. Civil order broke down as citizens declared war against a corrupt elite. In Thessaloniki, second city of the empire, a group calling themselves the "zealots" murdered the wealthy in their beds. In the countryside, the overtaxed peasants often welcomed the Turks when they came.

Constantinople had shrunk to a population of fifty thousand from perhaps half a million in its prime. With much of the city now farmland, it could feed itself from within its walls. By 1348, its annual income was little more than a tenth of that of Galata, the Genoese enclave across the Golden Horn. Just a century later, Galata's revenues would be seven times those of the entire empire.

Their empire might be shrinking, but the loyalty of ordinary Greeks to the Orthodox faith remained remarkably unshaken. One emperor after another went on bended knee to the Pope, offering subjugation to Rome and conversion to its creed in return for a crusade against the Muslim menace. In 1439, John VIII returned from Florence like Chamberlain from Munich: at last he'd managed to ratify the union of the churches, and he had the paper to prove it. But his people were having none of it. Their hatred of Rome surpassed even their hatred for the Turk.

Two thousand years of Greek and Roman empire were drawing inexorably to an end. But in Greece itself, where it had all begun, one last remarkable renaissance would hold the stage before the final curtain fell.

Mediterranean Camelot

It was ushered in by the French. On his way to join the Fourth Crusade, a Norman prince called Geoffrey Villehouardin and a handful of Frankish knights were blown by a storm onto the western coast of the Peloponnese. By 1213, Villehouardin ruled most of the peninsula. His palace at La Cremonie in the Vale of

Sparta became a byword for romance and courtly love. Knights would stop off there on their way to join the Crusades. In 1249, his son William built a great castle on a hill above to fend off the Slavic tribes still at large in the Taygetos mountains. This was Mystras.

A 17th-century view of Mystras by the Venetian cartographer
Vincenzo Coronelli

Not long before retaking Constantinople from the Latin Crusaders in 1261, the Greeks had reconquered the Peloponnese. The castle of Mystras became the citadel for a beautiful new city that slowly took shape down the steep slopes of the hill. The wealthy of Constantinople, realizing that the capital was doomed, decamped en masse to the new hilltop stronghold. They paid for many glorious churches, monasteries, and palaces, often built with stones taken from nearby Spartan ruins.

This Mediterranean Camelot was ruled by sons or brothers of the reigning emperor. Though they were known as *despotes*, the title did not carry the contemporary connotation. These were cultured, tolerant men, and they presided over a golden century of art and philosophy.

Plethon

Georgios Gemistos Plethon (1360–1454) was the most celebrated of Mystras's philosophers. As the Ottoman noose tightened around the empire's throat, Plethon drew up plans for a full-scale return to Hellenic values, including worship of the old gods. He took inspiration from both the Spartan and the Athenian model, envisaging the Peloponnese as a self-sufficient island where land was evenly distributed amongst the people. It would be defended by a citizen army who paid no taxes, and nourished by farmworkers who did. The idea would never be tested.

At the 1338–9 Council of Florence, Plethon acquired an Italian fan base. He gave lectures on Plato to rapt audiences who until then had only known about Aristotle. Cosimo de' Medici was so impressed that he set up a new Academy to spread Plato's teaching. Plethon was one of many to transfer precious ancient knowledge to the West.

His own remains were also carried west, after being stolen from Mystras by another Italian fan, Sigismondo Malatesta, Lord of Rimini. Plethon's final resting place is in the Tempio Malatestiano cathedral in Rimini.

Mystras was the last bright candle to shine before Greece was plunged into a new Dark Age.

The Fall of Constantinople

In 1449, Constantine XI was crowned in the tiny cathedral at Mystras, kneeling before a congregation of dignitaries whose titles no longer held any meaning. Soon afterward he sailed to Constantinople in a Venetian ship, to organize its defense. His chief commander was the Genoese condottiere, Giustiniani Longo, who brought five hundred mercenaries from the island of Chios. Knights from all over Europe joined them, as if to make amends for what their forebears had done in 1204.

The Turkish siege lasted for two months. It was ended by two monster cannon, each 120 feet long, which brought down the great walls. Built by a Hungarian gunsmith, the cannon had been offered first to the Greeks. But the crown jewels were still in pawn, so Turks got them instead. Constantine died on the city walls, and Sultan Mehmed II entered the city on horseback, riding up the altar steps of Hagia Sophia, the vast, domed cathedral that had served as focal point for the empire for almost a millennium.

It was another seven years before the Ottomans got around to Mystras. When they did, there was no army to defend it, and the despot Demetrius, last of the Palaiologos line, surrendered without a fight.

The fall of Constantinople was the 9/11 event of the age. For the West, it seemed like the end of times. The Byzantine Empire,

A mid-17th-century depiction of the fall of Constantinople in 1453

however feeble and degenerate it sometimes seemed, had always been the last bastion against the threat from the East. Now there was nothing to stop Islam from reaching the gates of Vienna and beyond. Nor was it just a matter of European security; there was commerce, too. Constantinople had been the final stop on the Silk Road, the vital trade route starting four thousand miles away in China's capital of Chang'an.

Yet reports of Europe's demise were exaggerated. Before the century was out, the Portuguese would build a ship that could round Africa, opening up the Indian Ocean for maritime trade and conquest. Few guessed it at the time, but a new age of Western dominance was about to begin.

PART TWO

The Longest Sleep
1453–1830

Greek Loss, Europe's Gain

Under the Ottomans, the Greeks, like Endymion of the myth, fell into a long sleep, from which they would not wake until the dawn of the Enlightenment. Four hundred years is a long time to be asleep; it's how long ago the Mayflower set sail from England to America. For Greeks in the north and on some islands, it would be longer. For those in Asia Minor, you can add a whole extra century. What did they miss? Much that was good, including the Renaissance. Much that was bad, too, like the Thirty Years' War (1618–48), into whose murderous centrifuge whole nations would be sucked, never to return.

Many rich and educated Greeks fled to the frontiers not yet taken by the Ottomans, like Crete or the Ionian Islands (both Venetian). Or they went abroad, mainly to Italy, bringing useful things with them. Plethon's philosopher-student Bessarion became a Catholic cardinal and donated his library to Venice. Thus the Greeks' loss became Europe's gain—more ancient texts to be mined for wisdom, another wave of Hellenic influence to wash across Europe and supercharge its Renaissance.

The Polis *Abroad*

When the philosopher Plethon traveled to the Council of Florence in 1438, he found its citizens far more in touch with the ideas of the *polis* than his fellow Greeks. Florence's era of self-government began in 1293 when the merchant families wrested control of the city from the aristocracy. By then Greek émigrés from Constantinople had already found their way to Italy, bringing with them classical texts on political science.

Florence has been called the "Athens of the Middle Ages," and government posts were filled by lot. The ruling *signoria* (also

---

chosen by sortition) was, like the Council of 500 in fifth-century BCE Athens, the highest branch of government, responsible for preparing and enacting laws. The English word "ballot" derives from the Italian *ballotta*—the numbered balls drawn to select candidates at random. Sortition was also used in other Italian city-states and in the Iberian kingdom of Aragon, where it was called *la insucalacion* and used to fill civilian public offices.

None of these merchant cities came close to Athenian-style *demokratia*, but they were more democratic than those within the Greek Empire, where the *polis* had all but disappeared. The Greeks' pious attachment to Christianity, their conservatism, and their isolation from the rest of Europe prevented their own ideas from coming back to them.

Poorer Greeks for whom emigration wasn't an option—farmers, herders, and fishermen—were left with only their clergy, often barely literate themselves, to lead and educate them. In Constantinople, Patriarch Gennadius had little choice but to cooperate with the new overlords. He was tasked by the sultan with presiding over all the empire's Orthodox Christians, not just the Greeks. In his first pastoral letter, he exhorted his flock to gain salvation "by obedience and submission to the church and its protector." "Obedience and submission" meant paying up; the "protector" was the sultan. The Ottomans did not outlaw other religions; they taxed them instead.

Now that they had an empire to run, the Turks needed a functioning bureaucracy, and it was the Greeks who were best placed to provide it. Over the next centuries, the Phanariots, educated Greeks who lived in the Phanar district of Constantinople where the patriarchal palace was located, would become the most favored of the sultan's subjects.

In the countryside, the priests kept alive a measure of Greek identity, but money was always short and most were barely more educated than the peasants over whose souls they presided. The Orthodox Church was spared the upheavals, expropriations, and persecutions of the Reformation, but as a result felt no need to change. The priests taught their flock enough to follow the mass, and nothing more.

Yet life under the Ottomans was better than Greeks would later claim, at least to start with. Most of mainland Greece is mountainous, and existence had always been precarious. Ordinary people found solace in religion and superstition—as well as in the glorious memory of Constantinople, which featured in their songs and poems as those of their ancestors had once featured Troy. As long as they paid the Christian poll tax (lower than the taxes they had been used to under the Byzantine emperors), they were largely left alone to live and worship as they pleased.

And for some there was a way out, albeit a harsh one. Every four years the Turks would cast a net over the sultan's European territories to catch the best boys to train in the ways of Islam and service to the sultan. This *devshirme*, or "boy tax," played a crucial part in staffing the Ottoman administrative and military elite. From the day they left their families, those netted by the *devshirme* were the slaves of the sultan. But these

A 17th-century Janissary

slaves could rise to dizzying heights. There would be no fewer than eight grand viziers of Greek origin.

The *devshirme* furnished the crack soldiers of the Ottoman army—the Janissaries—and manned the empire's civil service, but there were also opportunities for enterprising Greeks outside its mesh. In the seventeenth century, an odalisque (harem slave) named Kösem—said to be the daughter of a priest from Tinos—rose to rule the empire for a time. No wonder some parents offered up their offspring for enslavement.

In the cities, the Greeks were left to their own devices. Generally there was an Ottoman governor, a judge, and a garrison. Ordinary Greeks, Muslims, and Jews lived side by side. The Greeks ran their quarters according to the old Byzantine system, with elected leaders responsible for public services such as education, though in reality provision was very limited.

The Greek islands took longer to fall to the Ottomans. When Constantinople was conquered in 1453, most were in the hands of either the Venetians or Genoese. The exception was Rhodes, ruled by the Knights Hospitaller, whose piratical ways and dangerous proximity to the sultan's territories ensured that their island was the first to go in 1522. In 1540 the Cyclades (except Venetian-held Tinos) were taken, and in 1570 Cyprus was lost. Crete held out until 1669, when it finally succumbed after a marathon twenty-one-year siege of the capital, Heraklion.

During the century and a half between taking Rhodes and Crete, the Ottomans learned the importance of trade. Traditionally theirs was a warrior culture, valuing conquest above all else. If they built ships, they were for war, not commerce. As they added the Greek archipelago to their possessions, the sultans began to rethink. Decrees from Istanbul ordered lenience. There was no *devshirme* on the islands, and taxes were lowered. An end was put to forced labor and peasants were allowed to buy their land and bequeath it to their children. The aim everywhere was to promote trade.

Nowhere was this more apparent than on the island of Chios. Just three miles from the Turkish mainland, its main export was mastic—known locally as "St. Isidore's Tears"—a gum that seeps from the bark of the mastic tree. For centuries under the Genoese, the island had done brisk business with the sultans, who used mastic to sweeten the breath of their harems. The Ottomans encouraged the Chians to take up where the Genoese had left off, and thanks to the sultan's tax breaks and other privileges, they prospered. Later they would bleed for it.

A Sea Change

The first Ottoman reversal came at sea. In 1571, just after the fall of Cyprus, the combined navies of Venice, Spain, and the Papacy (the Holy League) destroyed the sultan's fleet at the Battle of Lepanto, fought off the north Peloponnese coast. The Ottomans lost their aura of invincibility and their dominant position in the Mediterranean, but their landward expansion continued until 1683, when they were driven back from the walls of Vienna itself. In 1684, a twin counterattack by Austria from the north and Venice from the south ended with the Venetians taking back the Peloponnese. They then fought their way up to Athens, where on September 26, 1687, they shelled the Parthenon (more than a century before Lord Elgin removed much of its frieze) and occupied the city for a year until the Ottomans drove them out again. The 1699 Treaty of Karlowitz deprived the Turks of a large part of their European territory, but they were far from finished. In 1715, an Ottoman army retook the Peloponnese, leaving only the Ionian Islands still in Venetian hands.

Enter the Bear

Under Catherine the Great, the Russians now began to play a decisive part in both Ottoman and Greek fortunes. In the Russo-Turkish War of 1768–74, vast territories were ceded to Russia, giving it access to the Black Sea and the long-desired warm-water port for its navy. The sultan was forced to accept the humiliating terms of the Treaty of Küçük Kaynarca, by which the tsar was acknowledged as the rightful protector of the Orthodox faithful throughout the Ottoman empire. More important, Greek merchants could now trade under the Russian flag. In theory, this meant that the might of the Russian navy stood behind them.

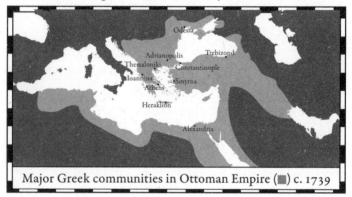

Major Greek communities in Ottoman Empire (■) c. 1739

Ever since Vladimir the Great had converted to Orthodoxy in 988, religious and cultural bonds between Russians and Greeks had been strong. Now the relationship was entering the realm of geopolitics too.

Greekness Rediscovered

It was from the borderlands and the islands, newly rich from Russia-backed trade, that the first sparks of the Greek Enlightenment came. For some time, Greek merchants had been building thriving communities along the trade routes into Europe: in

Vienna, Budapest, Belgrade, and other cities. These had their own schools and newspapers, and by the second half of the eighteenth century, educated Greeks on the fringes were beginning to admire the emerging European states, with their sense of nationhood based on shared history, language, and geography. They began to look back to an ancient, pre-Christian time, when Greeks, too, had shared a sense of national identity.

This process was helped by the Greek administrative class of Phanariots, who had come to wield considerable power as indispensable aides to the Turks. Some were now de facto rulers of the Danubian principalities (modern Romania and Moldova) and many were enlightened patrons of Greek culture, their courts conduits for western ideas. New academies in Ottoman cities such as Bucharest and Iasi became centers of Greek education and culture.

On the islands, meanwhile, thanks to the new trading dispensation, a booming ship-building industry had grown up by the early nineteenth century. Three islands in particular—Hydra and Spetses off the east coast of the Peloponnese, and Psara in the eastern Aegean—were constructing ships that could trade over long distances, which meant they had to be armed. Later their merchants would make fortunes running the British blockade of Napoleonic Europe, and after that would man the Greek revolutionary navy in 1821. For now, though, they were seeing for themselves in western ports just how far behind the Ottoman Empire had fallen.

Weakness at the Center

By the eighteenth century, the revenues of the king of France were ten times those of the entire Ottoman Empire. The Turks had always relied on conquest, not just for material plunder but for skilled manpower, too. With a culture still inflected with the traditions of their not-so-distant nomadic forebears, they didn't evolve the mechanisms needed to generate their own wealth. In the fifteenth century, northern Italians had invented modern banking; in the sixteenth, the Dutch had made bills of exchange transferable, creating vast new capital flows and opening trade routes across the world. With its clumsy command economy and antiquated financial system, the Ottoman Empire couldn't compete.

A string of weak sultans made the problem worse. As the tide of conquest subsided and the rot was exposed, there was no one to impose change. Again and again the coinage was debased, and the Sublime Porte (the Ottoman government, named after a palace gate) had to resort to tax farming to generate desperately needed revenue. On the Greek mainland, this business fell into the hands of local Primates (often Christian) who ruthlessly plundered the people and turned themselves into powerful warlords. The most egregious was the Albanian Ali Pasha, who by the late 1700s controlled huge territories in the northwest.

To escape the tax farmers, desperate men retreated into the mountains to become *klephts* ("bandits" or "thieves," as in kleptomania) while others took to the sea to prey on the busy shipping lanes of the Peloponnese. Or they emigrated. In 1675 alone, 430 members of the Stefanopoulos clan left the Mani—the central finger of the Greek Peloponnese—for Corsica. Some believe they are the ancestors of Napoleon Bonaparte.

Early Philhellenes

Beautiful architecture, perfected sculpture, painting, good music, true poetry, even philosophy itself . . . all this came to nations only through the Greeks.

Voltaire

For two centuries after the fall of Constantinople, few Europeans visited mainland Greece. The western contempt that had fueled the sack of Constantinople in 1204 had barely abated. Besides, as part of the sultan's empire, it was enemy territory. Now, though, the term *philhellene* ("lover of Greece") started to gain currency. Originating in France, philhellenism grew in popularity as the Enlightenment advanced, as it dawned on northern Europeans everywhere that they might owe more to Greek science and philosophy than to the inventions of the Romans.

When the Napoleonic Wars made Rome off-limits to travelers on the Grand Tour, they began to head to Greece instead, giving wealthy travelers like the Duke of Buckingham and Chandos the chance to bring home spectacular souvenirs, in his case an entire temple to adorn his country estate at Stowe. Meanwhile, Lord Byron's poetic blockbusters fanned a flickering passion for all things Greek into a blaze.

Disappointed Philhellenes

My respect for their name intensified my sense of their debasement.
Auguste de Choiseul-Gouffier in the 1770s

Yet very often, on seeing the fabled land up close, these long-distance philhellenes were disappointed. The people they met seemed to bear little resemblance to Pericles and his kind. Athens was a mean little town of fewer than ten thousand inhabitants, whose filthy streets were thronged with a decidedly unheroic mix of impoverished Greeks, Turks, and Albanians. Above them were the almost unrecognizable ruins of the Parthenon, parts of which were being chipped off daily to be sold to tourists who couldn't afford to ship a whole temple home.

Athens before independence

If the Grand Tourists had visited the culturally sophisticated borderlands, islands, or Constantinople, rather than just Athens, they might have found things more to their liking. This omission sowed the seeds of the Western idea that the modern Greeks bore no resemblance to their ancient counterparts.

Elgin Marbles

In 1801, Thomas Bruce, 7th Earl of Elgin and ambassador of King George III to the Sublime Porte, arrived in Athens. He claimed to possess an official firman from Sultan Selim III, authorizing him to survey and make casts of various ancient monuments—and to take away with him any pieces of interest.

Today, Elgin is infamous as one of history's great asset strippers, but it's more complicated than that. It remains an open question whether there really was a firman, but Elgin's motives may have gone beyond the lavish adornment of his Scottish pile. He bankrupted himself over the expense of getting the Marbles to London, and if they'd remained in place on the Parthenon, it is quite possible they would not have survived the Greek War of Independence, when the Acropolis was twice besieged.

None of this is to say that the Marbles should stay in the British Museum. As the Statue of Liberty proclaims American liberty, so the Parthenon represents Athenian democracy. Pericles built it, not just as a temple to Athena, but as an architectural celebration of the political system the Greeks had invented, and the Marbles are at the very heart of this celebration. In the words of the film star turned culture minister Melina Mercouri, they are the "essence of Greekness."

The campaign to repatriate them has attracted support from varied quarters, not all of it helpful. In 2014, George Clooney suggested they should go back to the Pantheon, a building in Rome. In 2019, an even more dubious ally emerged in Xi Jinping. During a visit to the birthplace of democracy, China's totalitarian leader declared: "Not only will you have our support, but we thank you because we, too, have a lot of our sculptures abroad." Perhaps not coincidentally, it was Lord Elgin's son who ordered the destruction of Beijing's Old Summer Palace during the Second Opium War.

There were thus two sets of Enlightenment torchbearers, who never compared notes because they were rarely in the same room: the western philhellenes from Europe and, later, America, and the educated, outward-looking Greeks of the fringes. The two groups tended to look to different parts of Greek history for inspiration. The Westerners harked back to the supposedly pure ideals of the Classical Age, while their Greek counterparts favored the spirit of pragmatism and compromise that had animated the Hellenistic and Byzantine periods. This split underpinned much disagreement to follow.

Enter Byron

In 1809, the twenty-one-year-old Lord Byron and his friend Cam Hobhouse visited Ali Pasha in his sumptuous palace at Ioannina in Epirus. Unaware that the romantic lake they gazed over positively brimmed with the bodies of tax-avoiding Greeks, the two fell hook, line, and sinker for the old psychopath's charms.

Tyranny notwithstanding, the city of Ioannina flourished under Ali Pasha as a center for Greek learning and culture.

The result of Byron's sojourn with Ali Pasha was *Childe Harold's Pilgrimage*, which made him world famous overnight. Though its brooding Romantic hero spent only a quarter of his travels among the Greeks, the poem recharged the West's obsession with their bygone glories—and their current enslavement by the heathen Turks. By 1810, minds all over Europe were starting to imagine the Greeks free from Ottoman vassalage.

Pressure Builds

Among the Greeks themselves, the picture varied. Around the edges of the Greek-speaking world, *Filiki Eteria* (the "Friendly Society") had been trying unsuccessfully to recruit revolutionaries for some time. Founded by three merchants from Odessa, they lacked a charismatic leader. Their top choice, Count Kapodistrias, serving as foreign minister to the tsar, had dismissed them as mere "wretched hucksters."

Meanwhile, on the islands there was little thirst for change. Treated differently by the Ottomans almost from the start, the inhabitants did not view their Greek identity or way of life as under threat. Nor did they feel isolated from the dynamic West; as shipbuilders and merchants, they were already part of Europe's economy. The low-tax, commerce-friendly regime had made them well-off, and most were content with the status quo.

It was on the mainland that the predicament of the Greeks was worst. Ordinary people groaned under taxation, lawlessness, and humiliating official discrimination, such as the ban on Greeks riding horses. For leadership they looked to the priests, who found themselves increasingly at odds with their superiors in Constantinople, where the patriarchy remained solidly behind the sultan. Pamphlet after pamphlet rolled off the printing presses to remind the faithful of Christ's injunction to obey the secular authority, but many local *papades* (priests) weren't convinced.

In the inhospitable Mani region in the deep south, where the law of vendetta held sway, anti-Ottoman feeling ran high. During the Russo-Turkish war of 1768–74, Catherine the Great had sent a fleet there in an attempt to provoke revolution. The rebellion had failed, and in revenge the Ottomans had unleashed their Albanian mercenaries. A nine-year reign of terror followed, among whose features was the grisly punishment of death by impalement. The Maniots hadn't forgotten.

Prophets and Martyrs

Ever since the Congress of Vienna drew a line under the French Revolution and its bloody aftermath, the Great Powers (Britain, Russia, Austria, and, later, France) had fiercely resisted democratization. Byron and others who saw the revolution as unfinished business found themselves dangerously at odds with their governments.

In 1793, the Thessalian writer Rhigas Feraios (pictured) traveled to Vienna to ask Napoleon Bonaparte to intervene on the Greeks' behalf.

While there, he published his *New Political Order*, which included a constitution, a map for a modern Greek-speaking commonwealth—and, of course, a battle song. But he was arrested by the Austrians and handed over to the Turks, who promptly strangled him and threw his body into the Danube. Sometimes described as the "proto-martyr" of the revolution, the story of Rhigas's death became as effective a call-to-arms as his song.

Adamantios Korais (1748–1843) was a different kind of radical. A scholar of ancient Greek literature and an intellectual to his core, he spent most of his life in Paris, where he witnessed firsthand the chaos of revolution. If Rhigas took inspiration from the French Revolution, Korais saw it as a warning. He looked further back to the customs of Classical Greece—including, infamously, its language. He was the inventor of *katharevousa*, the fiendish ancient-modern hybrid that remained the official language of Greece—and the bane of school-children—until 1976.

Korais was horrified by the backwardness of mainland Greek life and the ignorance of the clergy. He passionately believed that a classical education was the key to independence, though he didn't expect to live to see it, and his writings urged Greeks to build schools and libraries to promote national "regeneration."

The call was heard. By the start of the nineteenth century, the English traveler William Leake was able to report: "There is not a Greek community in a moderate state of opulence . . . that does not support a school for teaching their children the ancient Greek, and in many instances the other principal branches of polite education."

The Final Spark

In the second decade of the nineteenth century, earlier than Korais had expected, four things combined to spark revolution. First, in 1820, *Filiki Eteria* found a suitably dashing leader in Prince Alexander Ypsilantis, scion of a family of Phanariot princes in the sultan's Danubian provinces, who'd lost an arm in service to the Russian Tsar. Second, in January 1821, *Filiki Eteria* held a meeting at Vostitsa on the Greek mainland. It was attended by four bishops, including the dominant figure of Bishop Germanos. From then on, the all-important Church (except in Constantinople) was onside. Third, the merchants' ships, many of them armed, were lying idle now that the blockade of Napoleonic France had ended and a general postwar slump had set in. And lastly, Ali Pasha's crimes grew too heinous for his Ottoman overlords to ignore. He had all but declared independence, and the sultan's patience had run its course. In 1820, a Turkish army of twenty thousand marched north from the Peloponnese to confront him.

Thus, in March 1821, the Peloponnese was empty of its Turkish garrison.

THE GREEK REVOLUTION (1821–32)

Even with the sultan's army gone, surely it was madness. How could two thousand Greeks marching out of the Mani take on an empire of twenty-six million? Back in 1803, Adamantios Korais had thought he knew the answer:

> The Europeans . . . would repay with very great interest a capital sum received by them from the Greeks' ancestors.

Over time, as Korais had foreseen, the Greek revolutionaries would use their history to turn a Greek war into a European war.

Town squares all over Greece bristle with vastly mustachioed heroes of the Greek Revolution, each with three pistols and a *yataghan* (Turkish sword) poking out of his cummerbund. These men were indeed extraordinary fighters, but their lasting achievement was to gain time for less colorful Greeks to do their work in the chancelleries of London, Paris, and Saint Petersburg.

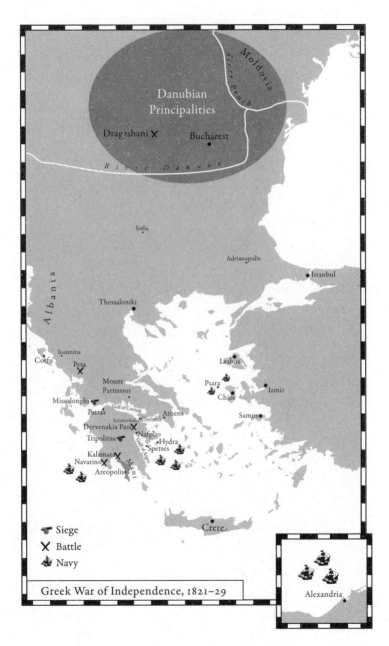

Danubian
Principalities

Moldovia

River Prut

Dragashani ✗   • Bucharest

River Danube

Sofia •

Adrianopolis •

Istanbul •

Thessaloniki •

A l b a n i a

Ioannina •
Corfu •   Peta
           ✗

Lesbos

Mount
Parnassus   Psara ⚓
                   Chios •
Missolonghi •   Izmir •
         Patras •   *Gulf of Corinth*
              Acrocorinth • Corinth • Athens •   Samos •
         Dervenakia Pass ✗
Tripolitsa ⚓ • Nafplio •
                   •Hydra
Kalamata •   M   Spetses
Navarino ✗   a
  ⚓   n   *Gulf of Argos*
      Areopolis • i

                        Crete

🔫 Siege

✗ Battle

⚓ Navy

Greek War of Independence, 1821–29

Alexandria

Their war drew on the spirit of Olympia rather than Sparta, and those who waged it were heirs to the diplomats who had staffed the Bureau of the Barbarians. They knew that Korais had been right: the only way Greece could win independence was with the help of the Great Powers.

Voyage of the Damned: Ypsilantis leads his student-troops to slaughter.

The Mani, at the southern tip of the Peloponnese, was a better place than Moldova to launch an uprising. Its fierce terrain and no less fierce people had never been properly conquered by the Turks, and if things went wrong there were plenty of places to hide. The Mani's three most powerful clans had always preferred feud to fellowship, but now they joined forces at Areopolis, the peninsula's tiny capital. This was the home of Petros Mavromichaelis, better known as Petrobey since he was the *bey*, or governor, appointed by the Ottomans to keep the Maniots quiet. As a plaque in the square testifies, he did not follow orders: "From this historic square was launched the great uprising under the leadership of Petrobey, March 17, 1821."

Further north, Bishop Germanos was heading for the port of Patras, and all over the countryside Greeks were rising up to begin a savage ethnic cleansing. At the start of March 1821, perhaps twenty-five thousand Turks farmed the Peloponnese. By summer, they had all either retreated into the coastal fortresses, or were dead. Soon after leaving Areopolis, Petrobey was joined by Theodoros Kolokotronis, scion of a famous *klepht* dynasty of whom it was said:

Petrobey rousing Messenia

On a horse they go to church
On a horse they kiss the icons
On a horse they receive communion
From the priest's hand.

Kolokotronis had obtained a modicum of formal military training during a stint with the British Army in the Ionian islands. Now he assumed command of the Greek forces in the Peloponnese.

The klepht

> *He will march, or rather skip, all day among the rocks,*
> *expecting no other food than a biscuit and a few olives,*
> *or a raw onion; and at night, lies down content upon the*
> *ground, with a flat stone for a pillow . . . he will submit to*
> *no discipline, for he thinks it makes a slave of him; he will*
> *obey no order which does not seem to him a good one, for*
> *he holds that in these matters he has a right to be consulted.*

Samuel Gridley Howe, American philhellene doctor, who fought and healed with distinction throughout the war (and whose wife, Julia Ward, composed the "Battle Hymn of the Republic")

Forced into mountain brigandage by the predations of the tax farmers, the *klepht* became the fearsome backbone of the Greek

> revolutionary forces. Lamb Klephtiko is still a favorite dish of the
> Mani: the meat is cooked with potatoes, vegetables, and herbs,
> and was traditionally prepared in a hole in the ground to stop the
> Turks from seeing the smoke.

After a bloody victory at the town of Kalamata in April 1821,
Petrobey issued the revolution's first appeal to the world. It ended
with the words:

> With every right does Hellas, our mother, whence ye also, O
> nations, have become enlightened, anxiously await your assistance.

Here was Greece explicitly asking Europe to repay the debt it
owed for the Enlightenment. This had been Korais's message, and
it now became the leitmotif for the entire war.

In the summer of 1821, Kolokotronis laid siege to the Ottoman
headquarters of Tripolitsa in the central Peloponnese. When the
town fell, he put some thirty thousand Turks and Jews to the sword
and enslaved the rest. Later that year, he marched on Nafplio. With
their army tied up fighting Ali Pasha, the Ottoman authorities
responded by blaming the man in Constantinople they'd ordered
to keep the peace. The elderly patriarch, Gregory V—hardly a friend
to the rebels—was dragged from his palace and hanged from its
gates with a placard around his neck. The ancient, scrawny prelate
took an age to die, but no one dared intervene. Soon afterward, a
hundred prominent Greek officials were publicly beheaded.

Enter the Phanariots

Petrobey and Kolokotronis were both regional warlords, but the
Greek cause also included members of the Phanariot caste, men
of education and wealth, some of whom had occupied positions

of privilege in the Ottoman Empire as civil servants, administrators, even princes. At first, the warlords welcomed them as the means to win over the Great Powers.

One of the earliest Phanariots to arrive was Prince Dimitrios Ypsilantis, fresh from serving with the tsar's Imperial Guard in Saint Petersburg (and as yet unaware of his brother's shambles in Moldova). A few months later, in August, came Prince Alexander Mavrocordatos, who wore morning dress whatever the weather. He'd journeyed from Italy, where he'd been staying with the poet Percy Bysshe Shelley. Like the Ypsilantis brothers, he was the scion of a proud (and very rich) family of governors in the Danubian Principalities. He spoke fluent Italian and Turkish, read ancient Greek, and understood English and French. He was a clever man—and, like Korais, he thought he knew how this war could be won.

Mavrocordatos and Ypsilantis set about creating the sort of government that would appeal abroad. In January 1822, the first National Assembly convened at Epidaurus in the Peloponnese. It was a site rich in useful associations. As sanctuary of Asclepius, the god of healing, and home to a vast, four-thousand-seat Hellenistic theater, it would have been familiar to any English milord who'd visited Greece on his gap year. The pair drafted a constitution of impeccable liberality, written in a Greek so archaic that no one without a classical education could understand it. It proclaimed the freedom of the press (Greece had no newspapers), the abolition of slavery (Greece had no slaves), and religious tolerance (there were very few Muslims or Jews left to tolerate). It had nothing whatever to do with reality, but it was perfect for foreign consumption.

A Fighting Navy

On the islands, meanwhile, the ships of Hydra, Spetses, and Psara had formed themselves into a kind of navy. But if the

Laskarina Bouboulina: widow, mother, shipping magnate, and naval
commander

klephts were unused to discipline, these island crews were in a
different class. They sailed under the ancient Oleron system,
whereby every crew member not only had a share in profits but
also a say in what went on. The jaws of British captains would
hang open at the sight of Greek crews refusing to leave port
without advance payment, or breaking off an action because
their contract had expired. Yet those same captains admitted that the Greeks were brilliant sailors, which the Turks
emphatically were not. They also had talented leaders, such as
Admiral Andreas Miaoulis, a Hydriot merchant, and Laskarina Bouboulina from Spetses, a ship-owning mother of four
who could drink her crew under the table. Despite the seeming
chaos, this island-navy played a critical role in supplying the
Greeks, harassing the Turks, and performing acts of derring-do
that played well in western drawing rooms, newspapers, and the
corridors of power.

Enter the Philhellenes

Through the summer of 1821, hundreds of Byron-besotted phil-hellenes, many of them veterans of the Napoleonic Wars, sneaked into the little ports of the Peloponnese. They expected a rapturous welcome, but the Greek commanders didn't know what to do with them. Many ended up simply wandering from village to village in search of an army to join, until their money ran out and their once splendid uniforms bleached in the Balkan sun.

An ex-Napoleonic colonel called Baleste found a use for some as officers over the few Greeks willing to accept the discipline of a regular army. But that still left many free to fill their days fighting ridiculous duels up and down the Peloponnese. Eventually, after Baleste had gone back to France in disgust, Major General Normann from Germany organized them into a single company.

Battle of Peta

It was a strange army that headed north in the summer of 1822 to confront the Ottomans, now rid of Ali Pasha and free to turn their attention to the Greek rebels. They were commanded by the singularly unmilitary Mavrocordatos, still in morning coat, with Normann acting as his chief of staff. Alongside the philhellene company and the irregulars were bands of *klephts* from the Peloponnese and the wild mountains of Epirus.

This motley two-thousand-strong force met some eight thousand Ottoman soldiers near the village of Peta in Epirus. Nothing showed the incompatibility of western philhellene and Greek *klepht* more clearly than the ensuing battle. The Europeans fired volleys and held their ground. The *klephts* fired from behind rocks then fell back. The Europeans were annihilated; the Greeks lived to fight another day. Mavrocordatos, humiliated, retreated to Missolonghi.

Word got back to Europe, and soon Marseilles was the only port that permitted young men to embark for Greece. There, a book by a disillusioned Prussian survivor named de Bolleman was doing the rounds:

> The Ancient Greeks no longer exist. Blind ignorance has succeeded Solon, Socrates, and Demosthenes. Barbarism has replaced the wise laws of Athens.

It wasn't long before Marseilles was closed too.

Counterattack

The Turks took revenge on their Greek subjects wherever they could. In early 1822, the sultan dispatched troops to prosperous, mastic-producing Chios, just off the Anatolian mainland, after hearing reports that the islanders had joined the uprising. In fact, men from nearby Samos had landed on the island to try to stir up rebellion, but the Chians had been hesitant. It didn't save them. The sultan's troops were soon joined by booty hunters from the mainland, and a terrible slaughter followed. By the summer, about three quarters of the 120,000 islanders had been killed or enslaved. Chios would never recover.

The only parts of the Peloponnese still held by the Ottomans were the coastal fortresses into which they'd retreated, but here, too, storm clouds were gathering. A twenty-thousand-strong Ottoman army was marching to relieve Nafplio, where the besieged garrison had been reduced to eating grass. The Greeks gave way before them, abandoning the huge citadel of Acrocorinth without a fight. Members of the government took to their ships, and the Gulf of Argos seethed with fleeing Phanariots.

Meanwhile, the Turkish fleet had set sail from Istanbul to join forces with the army when it arrived at Nafplio. In July 1822, the vanguard of the Ottoman army reached the town, broke the siege, and eagerly awaited the navy's arrival. But the Turkish admiral, harassed by the fleets out of Hydra and Spetses, refused to enter the bay and sailed back home instead. The Ottoman army was forced to try to escape through the narrow mountain passes where they'd failed to leave outposts on the way down. Kolokotronis and his *klephts* came into their own, ambushing the Turks at the Dervenakia Pass.

Civil Wars

The Greeks had retaken the Peloponnese and routed the Turkish army and navy. A second Assembly in February 1823 was meant to revise the constitution and set up a new government, but the divides proved insurmountable. The politicians thought they should control the military; the warlords thought the politicians should do as they were told and confine themselves to keeping their fighters supplied. Intoxicated with victory, neither side could yet see how much they needed the other. By 1824, free Greece had two governments: one official (the politicians, with support in the islands) and one rebel (Kolokotronis and the warlords).

Two brief civil wars followed, both in the Peloponnese. The first ended in July, when Kolokotronis surrendered Nafplio to the government. The second began in October, when a revolt against taxation gave Kolokotronis a chance to come back. The government persuaded the clan chiefs of central Greece, led by Ioannis Kolettis (a wily Epirot who'd once served as personal doctor to Ali Pasha's son), to march on their Peloponnesian brothers. Kolokotronis, devastated by the death of his son, surrendered. This time he was imprisoned.

Mavrocordatos had played his cards well by staying away from the infighting in the small western port of Missolonghi. It was a shrewd move, because Missolonghi was about to become the most famous town in Europe.

Byron and Friends

So far, the British had resisted Greek attempts to draw them into their struggle. But the most famous Briton of all was stirring from his lethargy. Lord Byron was now thirty-five years old, mourning his lost youth (and looks), and in a relationship whose spark had gone out. He was bored. So when an eloquent Irishman named Blaquière called on him in Genoa to suggest a Greek adventure, he leapt at the idea. He set sail for Missolonghi.

Before rousing Byron from his torpor, Blaquière had done something even better. He had presented the Philhellenic Committee in London with a prospectus for a large Greek loan to be raised on the London Stock Exchange. Much of the document was pure fiction: there was nowhere, it declared, with "a more productive soil, or happier climate, than Greece." But it worked. Nearly half a million pounds was on its way.

Mavrocordatos had calculated that Byron would have a big say in where the money went. So there on the quay to greet the English lord as he arrived at Missolonghi, late in the evening of Sunday, January 4, 1824, was a twenty-one-gun salute and a small, portly man in morning dress.

From the start, Byron loathed Missolonghi, soon discovering he'd come to a fetid, disease-ridden place of incessant rainfall.

> The dykes of Holland are the deserts of Arabia for dryness, in comparison.
>
> Byron on Missolonghi

The feuding Greeks all wanted to meet him, and it was impossible to know whom to trust. "There never was," he wrote, "such an incapacity for veracity shown since Eve lived in Paradise." He wasn't vain enough to think they loved him for his verse. They all thought he had the gold.

Mavrocordatos set about persuading Byron that the money should go to the true government of Greece, of which he was the representative, not to the warlords. But before the gold arrived, Byron caught a chill that turned to fever. On Easter Monday 1824, he died, just two days before the *Florida* docked with the first installment of the loan.

Trelawny's Cave

The British prime minister, George Canning, thought the Greeks "a most rascally set," yet it was an Englishman who was perhaps the biggest rascal of them all. Edward John Trelawny's background is obscure. He claimed Cornish descent, but then he also claimed to be a naval captain. What is certain is that he traveled to Italy in 1822 and there befriended Byron, who liked scoundrels, especially exotic-looking handsome ones who told good stories about their piratical adventures. Trelawny also managed to make friends with Shelley, teaching him to sail and helping to design the boat in which the poet would drown not long afterward.

Styling himself as Byron's agent, Trelawny fell in with the warlord Odysseas Androutsos, who owned a cave on the wild slopes of Mount Parnassus. The cave was enormous and very comfortable, with richly furnished rooms, enough supplies to withstand a lengthy siege, and, it was rumored, a huge hoard of treasure. Its mouth was sixty-five feet above the ground and could only be reached by rope ladder. A rampart and cannon defended it.

Odysseas entrusted Trelawny with the cave, along with his thirteen-year-old half sister, Teritza, whom Trelawny promptly took to wife. Two other Englishmen, Fenton and Whitcomb, were also resident. One day during shooting practice, seemingly egged on by Fenton for reasons that are unknown, Whitcomb shot Trelawny in the back as he inspected the target. Fenton was immediately killed by Odysseas's men, who then hung Whitcomb from the cliff face by his ankles.

With a bullet lodged in his spine, Trelawny endured an entire month of agony on a diet of raw egg, as prescribed by his teen-aged wife. Odysseas's men kidnapped a doctor and brought him to the cave to remove the bullet, but it proved too deep.

Eventually, Trelawny found his way back to England on a corvette, still accompanied by Teritza, though they divorced a few years later. Amazingly, he lived to the advanced age of eighty-eight, trading on his association with Byron and Shelley in a series of almost wholly fictitious memoirs. He was buried next to Shelley in Rome, Whitcomb's bullet still inside him.

The British gold reached the government at their headquarters at Nafplio. Mavrocordatos immediately used some of it to bribe the northern warlords to march south on Kolokotronis. The rest was largely squandered, but the Greek-versus-Greek fighting was over and the government now had in its ranks a man with the skill and experience to negotiate advantageous terms with the Turks. Unfortunately, the sultan was in no mood for peace. A powerful ally was on his way.

Enter Egypt

Egypt was a semi-autonomous province of the Ottoman Empire. Its *wali* (viceroy) Muhammad Ali, like Ali Pasha of Ioannina, was Albanian. The son of a tobacco merchant, he'd risen to high rank in the Ottoman army and helped kick Napoleon out Egypt. He'd also defeated the powerful Mamluk warrior caste, a thorn in the side of the sultans for centuries. With Istanbul's grudging approval, he had then established his own Egyptian dynasty.

In early 1825, Ibrahim Pasha, his heir, was sailing for Greece at the head of the biggest armada the Mediterranean had seen for centuries.

War of Extermination

The Greeks were relaxed. After all, they'd just beaten the Turks. But the Egyptian army had been thoroughly modernized by the French, whose newly restored Bourbon monarchy was eager to help anyone who'd bested Napoleon. And Ibrahim himself had plenty to gain from victory. Nominally he was sailing to the aid of the sultan, but he knew that if he could conquer the Peloponnese, it would be his to rule.

Ibrahim took the port of Navarino, then marched inland to Tripolitsa. His army destroyed everything in its path. As the historian and philhellene volunteer George Finlay put it:

> The Egyptians carried on a war of extermination; the Greeks replied by a war of brigandage.

The *klephts* fought on as their olive trees burned, and Kolokotronis was hurriedly released from prison to help lead the resistance. But as thousands fell to the disciplined Egyptian volleys, even he began to glimpse that they might need some outside help.

Act of Submission

So it was that, in September 1825, Mavrocordatos sent an "Act of Submission" to London. Extraordinarily, it was signed by almost all factions.

> The Greek Nation places the sacred deposit of its liberty, independence, and political existence under the absolute protection of Great Britain.

This was a desperate move at a desperate hour and, as Mavrocordatos knew it would be, it was rejected. But it was out there, and it had gone to the people who mattered.

Britain was the right target. The key to winning the war was the sea, so it made sense to approach the world's greatest naval power. Post-industrial revolution London was awash with cash, and a second Greek loan, this time of £1 million, had been raised in February 1825. Britain had considerable financial skin in the game.

Missolonghi

Then there was public opinion. Ever since Byron's death, the British chattering classes, and most of Europe's too, had been gripped by events at Missolonghi. The town had been under siege for months, presenting a rare picture of Greek unity. Souliote *klephts* from Epirus fought beside men from the Mani, while Admiral Maioulis kept both supplied by sea. But in January 1826, having failed to take Nafplio, Ibrahim Pasha brought his army and navy to join the fight. He sealed off the lagoon with his warships, and began to bombard the town with his howitzers.

The starving Greeks resolved to break out by night, leaving only the old and sick behind. But the escape was detected, and sortie became slaughter. When the Ottomans broke into the city, the surviving Greeks, sheltering in the very house where Byron had died, blew themselves up.

Missolonghi was a human tragedy and a military disaster, but it inspired a masterpiece of propaganda at the very moment when it was needed. The great French painter Eugène Delacroix had already done his bit for the cause: at the Paris Salon of 1824 he'd presented his "Massacre at Chios" to a horrified French public. Now, in just six months, he completed his *Greece on the Ruins of Missolonghi*. The huge painting depicted a beautiful woman kneeling among the town's ruins with her arms open in entreaty. People queued around the block to see it, and its message was unmistakable: Greece Needs You.

Greece on the Ruins of Missolonghi by Eugène Delacroix. This image galvanized Western support for Greece.

Protocols...

Greece was indeed on her knees but, unbeknown to most Greeks, the first signs of outside help were stirring in an unlikely place. Russia's tsar, Alexander, had a deep fear of revolution—yet, since the Treaty of Küçük Kaynarca, he was also the defender of the Orthodox faithful. Rumors began to circulate that Ibrahim Pasha planned to replace the population of the Peloponnese with Egyptian settlers in a so-called "Barbarization Project." Were they true, or had Mavrocordatos indulged in some tactical fake news?

Whatever the truth, the St. Petersburg Protocol was signed by Russia and Great Britain in early April 1826. The two powers agreed to seek a deal with the sultan: Greek self-government and the transfer of all Muslim property in Greece to Christians, with, in return, an annual tribute paid to Istanbul. The sultan rejected the terms out of hand.

The wheels of diplomacy were turning, but the situation on the ground was still grim. The second British loan had been almost as badly spent as the first. American shipyards were commissioned to build two warships, but costs had spiraled and only one materialized: the frigate *Hellas* that would become the flagship of the Greek navy. In late 1826, Sir Richard Church arrived to take command of the army, while Lord Cochrane, a dashing naval hero of the Napoleonic Wars, led the navy. These two British experts would prove a complete waste of money. On April 24, 1827, they tried to relieve the besieged Acropolis and retake Athens. It was a fiasco. Between 1,500 and 2,000 Greeks died in a single day, more than on any other during the whole war.

In July 1827, Britain, Russia, and France turned protocol into treaty. The Treaty of London *seemed* to allow for armed intervention if the sultan refused to accept its terms, and a British envoy set off for Alexandria to try to forestall the new fleet that was bringing the reinforcements for a final Ottoman victory. He arrived three days too late.

The new Egyptian army that arrived at Navarino soon afterward was set on holocaust. It landed and pushed inland. As the burning began, Kolokotronis was characteristically defiant:

> This action with which you would terrify us, threatening to cut down and burn up our fruit-bearing trees, is not warfare; the senseless trees cannot oppose themselves to any one ... but we will not submit—no, not if you cut down every branch, not if you burn all our trees and houses, not leave one stone upon another. ... If only one Greek shall be left, we will still go on fighting.
>
> Kolokotronis to Ibrahim Pasha

It was the same message Churchill would send Hitler a century later—your savagery only makes us stronger—and it was pitch-perfect in giving voice to the dogged spirit that drove the Greeks on. Yet, also like Churchill, Kolokotronis didn't have much to back it up.

Codrington Arrives

The first the Greeks themselves, with the possible exception of Mavrocordatos, heard of the Treaty of London was when Admiral Codrington, commander of the British Mediterranean fleet, sailed a squadron into Nafplio harbor. From there he moved on to Navarino, where he was joined by squadrons from the French and Russian navies.

The combined Turkish and Egyptian fleets lay at anchor inside the bay. Ibrahim knew that the allies were in a tricky position. It was late September and they wouldn't be able to stay outside the bay once the winter storms set in. The treaty did not quite preclude military intervention, but its wording was ambiguous; the idea was not to start a new war but to enforce a truce—if necessary by "peaceful interference," whatever that meant. Ibrahim reckoned he just had to play for time and his army would finish the job.

Yet Codrington was not a man for ambiguity. He had fought at Trafalgar under Nelson and liked things straightforward. Moreover, he was a committed philhellene. All he needed was a casus belli.

Hastings and the Casus Belli

> No man ever served a foreign cause more disinterestedly.
>
> George Finlay on Hastings

Of all the philhellenes, Frank Abney Hastings was the most popular among the Greeks. He had risen to captain in the Royal Navy and fought at Trafalgar, before being dismissed for challenging to a duel an admiral who had shouted at him in port. He then offered his services to the Greeks, and soon won their respect both for his seamanship and his coolness under fire.

Hastings may have been a prickly soul, but under sail he was an undoubted genius. In 1824, though, convinced that the age of steam had dawned, he returned home to build a new kind of ship, paid for mostly from his own pocket.

The *Karteria* featured on Greek 150-year anniversary stamps

This was the 230-ton *Karteria* (Greek for "perseverance"), a sail-steam hybrid. It was designed to sail into battle, then use its two huge steam-powered paddles to maneuver while its eight deck-mounted, sixty-eight-inch howitzers blasted red-hot incendiary shot at anything that would burn.

On September 30, 1827, Hastings sailed the *Karteria* into the Bay of Itea in the Gulf of Corinth, where ten Turkish ships lay at anchor. Switching to steam, he turned the ship in rapid circles while its giant cannon roared in all directions. Within an hour, four enemy ships had been burned and two captured. It was the first time that a steamship had fought in battle, and Hastings had emphatically proved its worth.

A year later, he died from his wounds while trying to retake Missolonghi. The Greeks gave him a state funeral, and his heart was removed, to be preserved in the Anglican church in Athens. There are many streets that carry his name in Greece—the Anglo-Saxon surname is usually rendered as *Astiggos*—yet he is virtually unknown in Britain.

Hastings Remembered: a Greek postcard issued on the centennial of his death

Provoked by Hastings's action, Ibrahim took advantage of the absence of the allied fleet, which was resupplying in the Ionian islands, to slip a squadron out of the bay and head north to the Gulf of Corinth. It wasn't much (and it was forced back by bad weather) but it was just enough to give Admiral Codrington his casus belli.

The Battle of Navarino

On the calm morning of October 20, 1827, three squadrons of British, French, and Russian men-of-war—twenty in all—sailed slowly into the Bay of Navarino, where a far larger Turkish and Egyptian fleet was waiting in perfect crescent formation to receive them.

What impelled Codrington to take such a colossal gamble? First, he believed he would win, however outnumbered he was. He knew what superior gunnery could do. Second, he was satisfied that he had the casus belli he needed. Most of all, he knew he'd be forgiven back home for ignoring the treaty's small print—provided he won. The British public had a financial as well as an emotional stake in an independent Greece.

As the allies cruised in with their gunports half open, Codrington's flagship dropped anchor dead center. Its brass band beat out its peaceful intentions, but not all the Turks were convinced. Inevitably, a nervous trigger finger slipped, and the music was quickly drowned out by the first deafening broadside. Over the next four hours, the two Ottoman fleets were blown to smithereens. It was the last naval battle fought under sail.

The Greek Revolution was won that afternoon. It would take another five years and a French expeditionary force to expel Ibrahim Pasha from the mainland, but after Navarino victory was inevitable. The Greeks had ensured that the Turks would be fighting not just them, but all of Europe.

PART THREE

The Rise and Fall of
the Great Idea
1830–1949

A Formidable Task

In February 1830, the London Protocol established Greece as an independent, sovereign state, only the second country in the world to gain independence from an imperial power. America, the first, had been left some infrastructure by the British. For Greece, the job would be much harder.

> [It was a] formidable task . . . to create a modern European state in a rather primitive region of the world, inhabited by an illiterate population of subsistence farmers who were preyed upon by disgruntled warlords, demobilised fighters and assorted brigands.
> Stathis Kalyvas, Gladstone Professor of Government,
> Oxford University

The biggest problems were size and money. With a population of just eight hundred thousand, Greece needed more tax-paying Greeks to evolve into a modern state, and two thirds of them still lived outside her borders. Everything depended on expanding those borders—and, of course, harnessing Great Power support to achieve it.

That support was far from guaranteed. Wellington and others wanted the Greeks to shut up for a while to give the conductors of the new Concert of Europe time to gather up their batons. Romantics with Byron still in their hearts didn't much care about things like borders. They just wanted the Parthenon to radiate liberty down from the Acropolis.

Some prescient observers saw the young nation as a laboratory for the new style of European politics. Greece was a pioneer of modern representative democracy, as she had been of the direct sort in ancient Athens. And with no conservative landowning class to get in the way, she would take strides denied other

European states, granting near-full male suffrage seventy-one years before Britain. She would give birth to some of Europe's first political parties, as well as a constitutional monarchy that formed half of one of the great political double acts in modern history. As the century went on, this newly minted democracy would morph into a dynastic oligarchy that would take Greece first to glorious triumph, then terrible failure. Much would be learned from the triumph; less from the failure.

The Retiring Count

All that was to come. For now, the price of Greek independence was actual control over her own affairs. From the moment the ink was dry on the London Treaty, the Greeks were subject to the whims of the Great Powers, particularly of their chief creditor, Britain. The new country's first leader had to be acceptable to those powers. Count Ioannis Kapodistrias, late of the tsar's Foreign Ministry, was invited to take up the role.

As soon as he landed at Nafplio in January 1828, Kapodistrias saw that his task was Herculean. The warlords had fought for regional power, not a nation-state, and they resented the imposition of central law and taxation on their fiefdoms. They loathed Kapodistrias, an ascetic, cosmopolitan workaholic who happened to be Greek, and he loathed them back.

Kolokotronis was the crucial exception. Kapodistrias might have seemed his besuited antithesis, yet the old warlord supported him for the same reason that many ordinary Greeks did: because he was clearly devoted to their cause. He rose at five and worked until midnight, building schools, distributing land that had been taken from the Turks, and negotiating to secure as much territory as possible in the peace treaty with the Sublime Porte in Istanbul. The new nation that emerged in 1832 included the whole of the Peloponnese as well as a strip of land north of the isthmus running from Arta to Volos.

But the mutual loathing between the other warlords and Kapodistrias never went away. On the morning of September 27, 1831, outside the little church of St. Spyridion in Nafplio, it was expressed in lethal Maniot fashion. Petrobey, who had first raised the standard in the tiny square of Areopolis a decade before, had been imprisoned on suspicion of stirring up revolt. Now his brother and son waited for Kapodistrias outside the church. The count saw them, hesitated a moment, then walked on. He was shot dead. You can still see the bullet hole in the walls of the church today.

The new state collapsed into anarchy and the Great Powers were forced to step in. The royal houses of Europe were combed for an eligible king, and the job fell to Otto, the seventeen-year-old second son of King Ludwig of Bavaria. On February 6, 1833, a day of bright sunshine, the teenaged German monarch sailed into the bay of Nafplio (still the capital), escorted by twenty-five warships.

New nation, old scores: Maniot warlords murder Greece's first head of state.

He brought with him a fresh loan of £2.4 million, three regents from his native country, and three thousand Bavarian soldiers to act as their enforcers.

Under the Bavarians

The new king's rule was absolute. His Bavarian officers quickly built a modern, disciplined army to impose order—at the point of the bayonet if needed. No part of the country escaped, including the wild Mani, where artillery was soon dispatched to topple the towers of the *klepht* warlords.

Kolokotronis, for many the very embodiment of the *klepht*, was made an early example of the consequences of dissent. Contemptuous of the "Bavarocracy" from the start, he was arrested for conspiracy and sentenced to death. The king pardoned him, which had always been part of the plan, but the point had been made.

With no real autonomy in the cards at home, the Greeks turned their efforts to the outside world. It had been Archimedes of Syracuse who, in the third century BCE, had first described

Otto's Bavarian lancers charge Greek rebels.

leverage—the art of moving large objects using far smaller ones. Now Kolokotronis looked to Russia for help in carving out a Greek Orthodox commonwealth across the Balkans, while Mavrocordatos and his more populist rival, Kolettis, looked respectively to Britain and France.

As ever, the most powerful weapons in Greece's diplomatic armory were geography and the past. But which past—classical or Byzantine? The classical one had always had the stronger hold on the Western imagination. Now, shorn of its most radical idea—after all, it was with weapons, not democracy, that industrial Europe had conquered the world—it was refitted for the new nation.

Athens was made the capital and bulldozed to create, piece by piece, a pastiche of its ancient namesake. Two thousand years of inconvenient civilization were swept aside to make way for buildings in the neoclassical style* to line the fine new boulevards. The Acropolis was cleared of its ramshackle village, including a Frankish tower and a mosque inside the Parthenon. The Bavarians flirted for a while with the idea of building Otto's palace on its summit but thankfully were dissuaded. Today the former royal residence houses the Greek parliament.

Education was enlisted in the service of this classical renaissance. In 1834, Greece was one of the first countries to introduce compulsory education, and students were taught in the hybrid ancient-modern form of Greek known as *katharevousa*. Three years later, the University of Athens was founded and a new subject—archaeology—was coined to unearth more evidence of past glories. Soon, young Greeks with trowels joined the Europeans digging among the ruins of Olympia, Delphi, and Messene.

---

* In northern European nations, neoclassicism signified an allegiance to universal Enlightenment ideals of reason and progress. In Greece it was about creating a national style.

Few of Otto's subjects knew much about, let alone revered, this ancient past. Kolettis insisted that Greece's capital should be Constantinople or nothing, and many ordinary Greeks agreed. Over the centuries, their customs, songs, and church rituals had kept alive the memory of a time when Constantinople had been Queen of Cities.

Even back in Bavaria, Otto continued to sport Greek costume.

From the start, Otto was caught between sponsors and teammates—between the circumscribed classical version of Greece espoused by the Great Powers and the expansive Byzantine nation dreamed of by his countrymen. When revolts against Turkey broke out in Thessaly and Crete in the early 1840s, he plumped for his Greek compatriots, even donning the *klepht*'s traditional uniform, the fustanella, to display his ardent patriotism.

The problem was money. There weren't enough taxpayers to sustain the existing state, let alone create a bigger one. Every year Greece had to ask the Great Powers for fresh loans just to keep up the interest payments on her existing debt. And these were the same Great Powers who emphatically didn't want her to get bigger. A bigger Greece meant a weaker Turkey, and that meant a stronger Russia.

To rein in the expansionist ambitions of the young nation and its monarch, the Great Powers cut off the money supply. Otto was forced to agree to unpopular austerity measures, while his foreign creditors took direct control of the tax revenues.

The Greek army, urged on by disgruntled politicians, now took matters into its own hands. In September 1843, a group of officers marched on the palace and presented a list of demands through a window. Otto could keep his throne but he'd have to rule under a new constitution. The rest of the Bavarians—sergeant majors and all—could pack up and go home.

To the City!

The constitution was ready by March 1844. On paper at least, it made Greece one of the most progressive liberal parliamentary democracies of its day, extending the franchise to almost all Greek male citizens.

The first political parties were gathering around war veterans like Kolettis, who relied on a system of patronage that went back to Ottoman times. Such parties were perfect platforms from which to broadcast the message of expanding the homeland to the huge new voter base. And their leaders knew there would be a democratic mandate for doing so—whatever the views of the Great Powers might be.

After decades of bitter factional rivalry, it must have seemed a good idea to delegate the business of running the country to the wisdom and experience of elected representatives, peacefully competing every few years for the public vote. But over time, distancing voters from government in this way would make them vulnerable to the siren song of populists. In the end it proved a short step from representative democracy to nationalist overreach.

Great Idea

In early 1844, the seventy-year-old Ioannis Kolettis, dressed as usual in the kilt of his native (and still Ottoman-ruled) Epirus, rose to speak in the new Assembly:

> Through her geographical position, Greece is the center of Europe, standing with the East to her right, and to her left the West. She was destined to enlighten, through her decline and fall, the West, but through her regeneration the East. The first of these missions was accomplished by our forefathers, the second is now assigned to us.

This was the first mention of what would become known as the *Megali*—or Great—Idea. The ambition—no less than the "enlightenment of the East"—was as vast as it was ill-defined, as much or as little as a politician chose to make it. But one thing was certain: at its very core was Constantinople. Soon crowds in Athens were crying, "To the City!" The Great Powers shook their heads and wondered how they could justify an intervention, given the all-too-evident will of the Greek people.

The Crimean War gave them the pretext they needed. In 1853, Russia and the Ottoman Empire went to war again, this time over the strategically vital Crimean Peninsula in the Black Sea. The Greek government, betting on Russian victory—and more land when the spoils were divided—came in on the Russian side. They turned a blind eye as volunteers and brigands poured across the northern borders, and revolts broke out in Epirus and Crete.

In early 1854, Britain and France, unnerved by the prospect of a breakup of the Ottoman Empire, joined on the Turkish side. The Greeks now found themselves at odds with two powerful sponsors, who wasted no time in demanding their withdrawal from all

Ottoman territory. When Otto refused, Piraeus was blockaded and the king was forced to back down.

Russia lost the Crimean War, and Otto his last shred of popular support. His ministers gave up any lingering illusion as to what independence actually meant. The Great Powers would never be brought around to the Great Idea as long as they saw Greece only in the image of ancient Athens. It was time to remind them, and Greeks themselves, of a different past.

Back to the Future

The Germans, who had done so much to resurrect the classical past, now proved ironically helpful in reviving the more recent Byzantine one. A schoolteacher named Jakob Philipp Fallmerayer set out to prove that the Greeks bore no resemblance to their ancient forefathers. Centuries of conquest had diluted their blood beyond recognition, and any talk of "rebirth" was therefore nonsense.

Fallmerayer paved the way for bringing the post-classical millennia into the modern Greek identity, but his racial definition of culture missed the mark. Another influential German, the philologist Kurt Wachsmuth, eloquently refuted the link between national identity and blood:

> A nation's essence and character lie in its language, its thought and sensibility, its whole style and civilization . . .

Konstantinos Paparrigopoulos, a professor of history at the new University of Athens, took up the baton. For him, too, the Greek nation was "all those people who speak the Greek language as their own tongue." His monumental five-volume history—perhaps the most important Greek intellectual achievement of the nineteenth century—told the full, *continuous* story of the Greeks, showing them to be heirs to two great civilizations, not one. From now on, it wouldn't be Athens or Constantinople, but both.

Greek Folklore

In the early nineteenth century, the Brothers Grimm had looked to German folklore, rather than race, to locate their country's *Volksgeist*. Now Greek folklorists like Zambelios and Politis followed their example, gathering the songs and stories that had entertained generations of illiterate Greeks. They collected the epic poems of the *Akritai*, the defenders of the borders during the Byzantine-Arab wars from the seventh to the eleventh centuries. The best-known was *Digenes Akritas*, which related the superhuman exploits of a heroic warrior:

They hissed like dragons, they roared like lions, they soared like eagles . . .
And from the great clashing and the cut and thrust
The plains grew fearful and the mountains re-echoed
Trees were uprooted and the sun was darkened.

They also gathered klephtic songs, many from Epirus, the wild, mountainous region of northwestern Greece. *Mirologia* (literally "words of fate"), perhaps Europe's oldest surviving musical form, are often sung extempore by women at funerals. Many feature Charon, the ferryman of Hades:

Why are the mountains black and welling up with tears?
Is it the wind that batters them, is it the rain that beats them?
It's not the wind that batters them, it's not the rain that beats them
It's only Charon going past, with the dead departed.

Otto's reign dragged on for another eight years. In 1861, he made the mistake of backing the Austrians against the Italians, who were seeking their own version of classical revival and nationhood. In the autumn of 1862, while he and his queen were touring the Peloponnese in the royal yacht, the army staged a bloodless coup. The couple were intercepted en route to Piraeus. Otto would never again return to Greece, though he continued to wear fustanella for the rest of his life. Meanwhile, the army had learned how easily it could change a government it didn't care for.

King of the Hellenes

It was time for a reset. Otto had routinely abused the constitution and the Greeks needed a monarch who'd abide by a new one that was even more liberal.

Who should this new king be? A referendum was held, and 95 percent of Greeks voted for Queen Victoria's second son, Prince Alfred, who had the advantage of hailing from the strongest and richest among the country's sponsors. But Greece was too geographically important for any of the Great Powers to tolerate the representative of another being in charge. Instead, the Greeks were given a Danish prince.

He turned out to be a good choice. King George, as he became, was happy to be bound by the new constitution. He also married the tsar's niece, which meant that his heirs would be of the Orthodox faith. Best of all, he brought with him the Ionian islands as a gift from Britain, which had taken them from France during the Napoleonic Wars. It was the country's first territorial gain since independence, and an implicit recognition that Greece in its current form was too small to succeed.

The direction of travel was clear from the moment George was crowned King of the *Hellenes* rather than of *Hellas*. The nation was no longer being defined by its boundaries, but by its people. The same was happening all over Europe. Although the 1848 revolutions, inspired by the triumphs of the Greeks two decades earlier, had been quashed, the genie of nationalism was out of the bottle. By the 1870s, the new states of Germany and Italy had brought their respective peoples within a single national boundary.

Why not Greece too?

Heinrich and Sophia of Troy

In 1869, Theokletos Vimpos, archbishop of Mantineia and Kynouria, was teaching Greek to an amateur German archaeologist in his Athens mansion. Heinrich Schliemann was forty-seven, divorced, and looking for a new wife who was "enthusiastic about Homer and a rebirth in my beloved Greece." He asked the cleric for help. The archbishop duly  presented three photographs of beautiful Greek women for Schliemann to choose from. Among them was Sophia, his own seventeen-year-old niece. Heinrich chose her.

Four years later, Schliemann was excavating a site in northwestern Turkey that he believed might be Homer's Troy, when he unearthed "Priam's Treasure," a fabulous hoard of gold jewelry and other artifacts. Soon afterward, photographs of Sophia Schliemann, adorned in Trojan finery and the very reincarnation of Helen of Troy, were flashed across the world to spark a new wave of philhellenism.

> Despite the thirty-year age gap, the Schliemanns' marriage
> seems to have been happy. They had two children named—of
> course—Andromache and Agamemnon.

Parties, Patronage, Polybius

Under the new regime, scores of small political parties emerged.
But beneath the democratic froth, familiar currents were at work
as powerful families used old patronage networks to manipulate
the system. In Polybius's cycle, citizen-based democracy was supposed to replace oligarchy, not coexist with it. Instead, Greece's
oligarchs were now finding ways to exploit the form of democracy
to further their own ends.

In May 1875, Charilaos Trikoupis became prime minister. He
ended the right of the king to appoint the government; from now
on it would be the leader of the party with the most parliamentary seats. It was a move that dented royal power but boosted that
of the oligarchy. Something like a two-party system formed as the
smaller parties duly merged, though it was based on personality
as much as on policy.

Greece's versions of Gladstone and Disraeli (Britain's great
nineteenth-century parliamentary rivals) were Trikoupis and Diligiannis, but with a crucial difference: Trikoupis was Mavrocordatos's nephew, and Diligiannis's uncle had been Kolokotronis's
lieutenant. Unlike their British counterparts, both were bound
to their voter bases by networks of kinship and patronage. These
were dynasties disguised as political parties.

Diligiannis is famously quoted as saying, "I'm against
everything Trikoupis is for." In fact, both men were emphatically
for the Great Idea; they only differed on how to realize it. While
Diligiannis clamored for war, Trikoupis wanted to strengthen the
existing state before venturing further afield. Nevertheless, it was

under Trikoupis that the second big expansion of Greek territory now took place.

Thessaly

The opportunity arose in 1877, when Russia once again went to war with the Ottoman Empire. As in the Crimean War, Greek irregulars crossed the northern borders into Thessaly and Macedonia, and there was an uprising against Ottoman rule in Crete. A year later, a hastily conscripted Greek army invaded Thessaly. At the Congress of Berlin (1878), the Great Powers agreed to let them keep it.

Fertile Thessaly was certainly worth having, but for most Greeks, fired up by their politicians, it was just the beginning. There was still Macedonia and its wealthy capital, Thessaloniki, not to mention the islands and—the ultimate prize—Constantinople itself. But the Great Powers didn't want any more threats to Europe's increasingly precarious equilibrium. For the time being, the door leading to the promised land of the Great Idea was firmly shut.

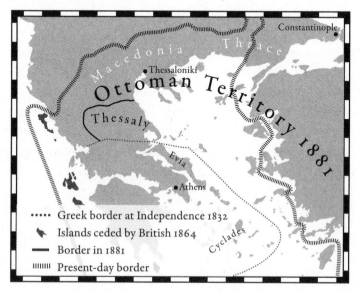

..... Greek border at Independence 1832
🐦 Islands ceded by British 1864
— Border in 1881
|||||||| Present-day border

The construction of the Corinth Canal, 1890s

"Regrettably, we are bankrupt"

Thus thwarted, the Greeks turned to grand domestic infrastructure projects they couldn't afford. After two millennia of trying (Nero himself had swung a pick back in 67 CE) the Corinth Canal was finally opened in 1893, linking the Aegean and Ionian seas and saving ships the stormy journey around the bottom of the Peloponnese.

It could only end one way. In 1893, Trikoupis rose in parliament to make the most famous announcement of his career: "Regrettably, we are bankrupt." It hardly seemed an auspicious time to stage the Olympic Games.

The First Modern Olympics

The first Olympics of the modern era were the brainchild of Pierre de Coubertin, a French aristocrat who, like the ancient Greeks, believed passionately in the uplifting effect of competitive sport, not just for participating individuals but for the world.

News that the first Games were to be held in Athens was greeted with wild enthusiasm by almost all Greeks. One exception was the cautious Trikoupis, who assented only on condition that the Greek government would foot none of the bill. So a campaign began, led by Crown Prince Constantine, to raise the money through public subscription, the sale of postage stamps, and the tapping of rich Greeks abroad.

A range of 1896 Olympics stamps raised funds for the Games.

On Easter Monday, the Games were officially opened by the king before a crowd of eighty thousand packed into the refurbished Panathenaic Stadium. The event would last six days, involve fourteen nations (thirteen European, plus the United States) and feature nine sports. They were emphatically amateur—the British team was staffed largely from the embassy in Athens—and run on a shoestring. Tennis matches were played at the Athens Lawn Tennis Club, and all swimming races took place in the notoriously chilly waters of the Bay of Zea.

Over 65 percent of the competitors were Greek, which explains their haul of forty-seven medals, more than double their nearest rival, the US. The most celebrated competitor will always be Spyridon Louis, the twenty-four-year-old shepherd who won the first marathon race in shoes that had been donated by his fellow villagers. As he entered the stadium, Princes Constantine and George leaped from their father's side to run alongside him over the finishing line.

Black '97

The Games had been a powerful symbolic reminder of just how much the West owed Greece. Surely now was the moment to realize the Great Idea. Huge crowds gathered in Athens to clamor for war with the Turks, and their call was heard by king and parliament. In February 1897, Prince George led an expeditionary force ashore in Crete to claim the island for Greece. The reaction of the Great Powers was swift and deflating. Instead of *enosis*, the island would be partitioned among Britain, France, Russia, and Italy.

Crete was a setback, but it wasn't enough to quell the national expansionist urge. In March 1897, a Greek army of fifty thousand marched across the northern border into Ottoman territory. It was all over embarrassingly quickly. The sultan's army had been modernized since the Russian war. It needed less than a month to send the Greeks scurrying back over the border, and went on to reoccupy the whole of Thessaly. Once again, the Great Powers stepped in, enforcing a truce and agreeing to Greek reparations that the Great Powers themselves had to pay. Thessaly was returned to Greece, but the International Financial Commission removed control of the economy from the national government. It was the nineteenth-century version of the EU's troika, sent in during the financial crisis to regulate Greek affairs. It was no less humiliating.

"Black '97," it was called, and the mood in Greece was indeed pitch black. On top of the pain of defeat and the shame of the

Commission was the dawning realization that the other peoples of the Balkans were now on the path toward their own Great Ideas. From now on they would be in competition not just for land, but for support from abroad as well. And the signs weren't good. Russia, for centuries an ally, had tilted toward a nationalistic "pan-Slavic" agenda, and was throwing its weight between Serbia and Bulgaria.

As the old century drew to its close, Greeks emigrated in the thousands, many into Ottoman territory. There was a spate of high-profile suicides, especially among the young. The new country seemed to be dying before it had really started to live.

New Century

The dawn of a new century was an opportunity to take stock, but most Greeks were in no mood for reflection. In the north, Bulgaria and Serbia were eyeing up Ottoman lands, especially Macedonia, just as eagerly as Greece was. Village by village, an undeclared war of coercion, extortion, and intimidation was being waged, with ordinary people forced to choose their ethnic and religious allegiance. The national mood of self-hatred began to change into hatred of all things Bulgarian.

Yet there was much to celebrate about the seventy years since the revolution. The Ionian islands and the rich plains of Thessaly had been won with the help of the Great Powers, who, while not actively encouraging the expansion of Greece's borders, were at least guaranteeing those that existed.

Politically, the all-consuming issue was whether the Great Idea should be pursued by force or diplomacy. The former approach seemed to have much in its favor. Hadn't Thessaly been won by the mere *threat* of force? And didn't every year of waiting just strengthen the hand of the Bulgarians and other Balkan rivals for Ottoman spoils?

Cautious onlookers were wary. They could see how the new politics, with two parties competing for the vote of an easily manipulated population every few years, were vulnerable to hubris and overreach. In theory the monarch served as a brake, but the new constitution had reduced the king's powers.

Young Turks

In fact, a temporary brake on Greek adventurism now came from another direction. In 1908, a group of junior Ottoman army officers in Thessaloniki staged what has become known as the Young Turks' revolution. The officers demanded democratic reform across the empire, and the message from Enver Pasha, their leader, resonated not only with the sultan's Muslim subjects but with the millions of Greeks who still lived in Ottoman lands.

We are all brothers. There are no longer Bulgarians, Greeks, Serbs, Romanians, Jews, Muslims—under the same blue sky we are all equal, we are all proud to be Ottomans!

Perhaps a version of the Great Idea could be realized within the Ottoman Empire? An Ottoman commonwealth, but a commonwealth nonetheless. It wasn't to be. The Balkans erupted (Bulgaria declaring independence, Austria annexing Bosnia and Herzegovina), and Crete again demanded *enosis* with Greece, only to be denied again by the Great Powers. Soon a backlash blew in from the east. The Young Turks changed their rhetoric from fraternity and multiculturalism to something more religious and nationalist, and more attractive to the millions living in the rural Anatolian hinterland.

With the Turkish leadership in turmoil, Ottoman Greeks feeling threatened in the new jingoistic climate, and Bulgaria (nicknamed the Balkan Prussia) rapidly arming, the time for action seemed to have come. But still the Greek king and government prevaricated. Black '97 had not been forgotten.

Enter Venizelos

The stage was set for the man many believe to be the greatest modern Greek to make his dramatic entrance. Eleftherios Venizelos was the charismatic leader of the Cretan struggle for *enosis*. Now a group of officers of the Athenian garrison, after overthrowing the government in a coup, turned to him for leadership. He came to Athens, founded the new Liberal Party, and stormed to power in the December 1910 elections. The Venizelos Era had begun.

In a blizzard of new legislation, government was streamlined and taxation overhauled. Landed estates in Thessaly were broken up and agricultural output boosted. British and French experts were brought in to reform the Greek army. By 1912, the economy was in surplus for the first time in the country's history, and there was money to spend on the Great Idea.

Balkan Wars

Venizelos (right) meeting Serbian Prime Minister Pašić in 1913

Venizelos's gift was to "combine the diplomatic skills and patience of a Mavrocordatos with the popular appeal of a Kolettis or a Diligiannis" (Roderick Beaton). Now he would parley with the very devil to get what he wanted. With the Turks diverted by war in Libya, he sat down first with Bulgaria, then with Serbia.

In October 1912, the three nations simultaneously declared war on the Ottomans. On November 8, Prince Constantine led his army into Thessaloniki to claim it for Greece just hours before the Bulgarians. Four days later, the king and Venizelos joined him to celebrate the greatest Greek victory since the revolution. In March of the next year, Ioannina, capital of Epirus, was taken. At a stroke, Greece had more than doubled her size.

For once, victory had been achieved without outside help, but the peace talks were held in London, with all the Great Powers present. This time, though, the Greeks were present too, in the person of Venizelos himself, who grasped the opportunity to

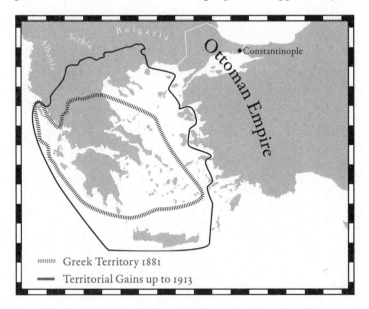

▭▭▭ Greek Territory 1881
▬▬▬ Territorial Gains up to 1913

arrange private audiences with David Lloyd George, chancellor of the Exchequer, and Winston Churchill, First Lord of the Admiralty. He came out of those meetings convinced that he had the blessing of the Great Powers to go all the way to Constantinople—and possibly even beyond.

Venizelos knew he could win a popular mandate for an eastern adventure, so long as the cautious King George didn't interfere. The king wouldn't get the chance. On March 18, as he was taking his morning stroll, he was shot at point-blank range by a young alcoholic, just six months short of his fiftieth year on the throne. A great political partnership had ended at the point when it was most needed.

A Winning Hand?

The new king looked like the perfect successor to his father. Constantine was fresh from victory, experienced, and married to the sister of the German kaiser, ruler of Europe's rising power. And he seemed to have been passed a winning hand. The Balkan Wars had redrawn borders greatly to Greece's advantage, and soon afterward Crete at last came into the fold, handed over by an exhausted Ottoman Empire at the Treaty of Athens. Constantine inherited a peaceful kingdom double the size and population of his father's at the time of his accession. He also inherited Venizelos, the man who'd brought the Great Idea halfway to fruition, and secured (so he believed) the support of the Great Powers to do the rest.

Powder Keg Blows

George's murder had shaken the Greeks, but the one that came a year later rocked the world to its foundations. In Sarajevo, on June 28, 1914, Archduke Ferdinand, heir to the Austro-Hungarian throne, was shot dead. This single act by a Serbian nationalist triggered the bloodiest thirty-year period in European history.

As the Great Powers plunged into the First World War, Greece's neutrality was agreed on as the rational course for a country whose king was married to the kaiser's sister, but whose prime minister was closely allied with Britain and France. War with Great Britain would surely be madness, given the Royal Navy's undisputed command of the seas. And there seemed little reason to get involved in a messy and expensive global conflict in which Greece was too weak to make a real difference.

Great Schism

It wasn't long before cracks began to show in the relationship between king and first minister. Over the next four years, they would deepen into a National Schism, with two governments, two capitals, and two armies presiding over two halves of Greece, and the country in a state of vicious, if undeclared, civil war.

Within weeks of the outbreak of war, Venizelos, encouraged by his secret "understanding" with the British establishment, offered to bring Greece in on the Allied side. The offer directly contravened the agreed-on policy of neutrality, and was made without even consulting the king. It was politely declined.

By January 1915, the Ottoman Empire had entered the conflict on the side of Germany and Austria. Bulgaria hadn't shown its hand, but with a formidable army of over a million men—around a quarter of its population—it now assumed vital strategic importance. If it declared for the Central Powers, it would provide an overland link between the Ottoman and Austrian Empires. In a bid to stop this from happening, Britain tried to persuade Greece to give Bulgaria some territory in exchange for a slice of Albania and a vague promise of gains in Asia Minor after the war. Venizelos wanted to accept. The king didn't.

The following month, February 1915, the Allies opened a new front against the Ottomans in the Dardanelles. Venizelos agitated for Greece to join the Gallipoli campaign. At first the king agreed, but when his risk-averse (and pro-German) chief of staff, General Metaxas, resigned, he changed his mind. Venizelos resigned, too.

Before long he was back, winning the June 1915 election. In September, Bulgaria finally came into the war on the side of the Central Powers, having made a deal with Turkey that would give it control of much of the Balkans if they were victorious. Venizelos once again defied official Greek neutrality by offering support to Serbia should Bulgaria attack. This time, the king dismissed him.

Venizelos now decamped to Thessaloniki. The city was the heart of the "'New Greece" where his power base was; it was also close to the new Macedonian front that the Allies had set up to help Serbia.

New Greece versus Old Greece

Greece was now at virtual civil war, with pro-Venizelos New Greece in the north and royalist Old Greece in the south. In June 1916, the Allies, mistrustful of the Greek army to its rear, sent a formal note to the king demanding that he disband it. Constantine had no choice but to obey.

In August, Venizelos formed his own government in Thessaloniki, with its own army. Greece now had two capitals, two governments, and two armies, disbanded or otherwise. In December, British and French troops marched into Athens to confiscate all weapons still held by royalist troops, and fighting broke out between Allied forces and Greek soldiers. Six months later, the Allies deposed Constantine, replacing him with his second son, Alexander. They also formally recognized the Venizelos government in Thessaloniki.

Constantinople's Greeks fly flags to welcome the Allied armies in 1919.

This was the most flagrant insult to Greek sovereignty so far. When Venizelos returned to Athens, he found Old Greece seething with resentment, not only against the Allies but against him personally as their stooge. His supporters launched a purge of royalists from the civil service, the courts, and the army.

In September 1918, the Allies, helped by nine divisions of the Greek army, broke through in Macedonia. For the first time in five hundred years, Greek soldiers marched into Constantinople. At long last, the Great Idea seemed within grasp.

Two Continents and Five Seas

As soon as the war ended, Venizelos raced to London. There his "inexhaustible eloquence" (Lord Curzon) won for Greece the whole of Thrace (excluding Constantinople), a large part of western Anatolia, and a mandate to occupy the coastal city of Smyrna and its environs, pending a plebiscite to decide the region's long-term fate—all under the 1920 Treaty of Sèvres. Greek forces had already landed, and now they pushed inland from Smyrna.

Venizelos surveys the *Greece of Two Continents and Five Seas.*

Venizelos returned to Greece a hero. His vision of nation had been gloriously vindicated, and something that looked like the Byzantine Empire was being reincarnated around the Aegean. The British politician Harold Nicolson described him as one of the "great men of Europe." Many Greeks agreed—but not all, especially in the south, and especially in the army. Nevertheless, he was so confident of his popularity that he invited the monarchist opposition back from exile to fight the 1920 election.

To general amazement, the opposition won. Perhaps it was resentment at the continuing violation of Greek sovereignty by the Great Powers. Perhaps it was the sudden death of King Alexander from a monkey bite and the return of his popular father, Constantine.

The new regime faced an immediate and difficult decision. What should they do in Asia Minor? A provisional Turkish government had been established in Ankara by Mustafa Kemal (later *Atatürk*). It rejected the Treaty of Sèvres and wanted the Greeks out of Turkey. Instead of backing their official mandate holder—Greece—the

Great Powers, unable to forgive what they saw as Constantine's betrayal during the war, withdrew their support altogether.

All of which makes it baffling that the king decided to press ahead with the Turkish invasion. He had no outside backing and his new government had specifically campaigned against it while in opposition. Perhaps he was swayed by the passion of the ordinary soldiers who hailed him as "Constantine XII"—successor to Constantine XI, last Emperor of Byzantium, who had died on the walls of his city in 1453.

The word Greeks still use today to describe what followed is *catastrophe*, and it is no exaggeration.

Catastrophe

The Greek army continued to push east. In the autumn of 1921, it met the Turks at Sakarya, just west of Ankara. The battle was closely fought, but the Greek advance was halted. A year of stalemate followed as the Turks gathered their forces for the counterattack. When it came, the Greek line held for only two days before the army fell into headlong retreat back toward the sea.

Civilians caught in the path of the armies—Greeks and Turks alike—were forced from their homes and often killed. Those Greek refugees who managed to make it to the coast at Smyrna found themselves trapped in a new kind of hell.

Infidel City

The Ottomans called Smyrna "Infidel Izmir" because more than half of its population was made up of Greeks, Armenians, Jews, and other foreigners. In May 1919, the city's long and multicultural history as one of the great trading centers of the Mediterranean came to an abrupt end when the Greek army summarily executed what was left of the Turkish garrison.

After the Turkish victory at Sakarya, Greek civilians from the interior fled west into the city. Half a million refugees crowded onto the waterfront, hoping to be rescued by ship. But the Allied commanders of the only ships to hand had strict orders to embark no one except their own nationals. Their crews looked on as women and children were picked off one by one by Turkish snipers.

It was a bloodbath. The Turkish army took its revenge, massacring over thirty thousand Greeks and Armenians, while a mob hacked the Orthodox archbishop to death. Then they set fire to the city. Four days later, only the Turkish and Jewish quarters were still standing. Buried in the ashes of Smyrna were not just the Great Idea, but 2,500 years of Greek civilization in Asia Minor.

Perhaps a quarter of a million Greeks were killed in the battle for western Anatolia. The dream had turned into a nightmare. Who was to blame? The returning army was in no doubt. They demanded Constantine's abdication and the resignation of his entire government. Five senior politicians and the army's chief of staff were summarily tried for high treason, found guilty, and shot by firing squad. Over the next two decades, the Trial of the Six would become the festering wound that goaded Venizelos's enemies.

The Prince and the Fruit Crate
In the months after the Anatolian disaster, Athens resembled the Paris of Robespierre. The Revolutionary Tribunal set up for the Trial of the Six also brought before it Prince Andrew, youngest son of Constantine. His crime was to have disobeyed an order to send his army corps into the attack on the battlefield of Sakarya.

His defense was that he had refused to put his men's life at risk for a pointless exercise.

The tribunal found him guilty and he only narrowly escaped execution. Instead, he and his family were sent into exile. His youngest child and only son was blissfully unaware of the drama, being just eighteen months old at the time. Philip was carried on board the waiting British destroyer in an orange crate, a humble cradle for a man who would later marry the queen of England.

Churchill blamed the catastrophe on the monkey that had bitten Alexander and brought King Constantine back to Greece.

> It is perhaps no exaggeration to remark that a quarter of a million persons died of this monkey's bite.
>
> Winston Churchill

Without Constantine back on the throne, the logic went, the victorious powers would have stepped in to prevent Greece's defeat. It's a moot point. They were already stretched thin with other mandates across the world.

Others have blamed Venizelos for deluding himself that the Asia Minor enclave could have been held against the Turks. Hadn't the *akritai*, the frontiersmen of the Byzantine Empire, found the eastern border impossible to defend? Surely it would have been only a matter of time before the far more numerous Turks reclaimed their territory. Wouldn't Constantinople have been a more realistic target, with the Bosphorus as the natural boundary between Europe and Asia? The Great Powers might even have been amenable; after all, any talk of "Tsargrad" had ceased since the Bolshevik takeover of Russia.

Perhaps the fault ultimately lies with a political system that tends fatally toward populist extremes. Since independence,

Greece had followed Polybius's cycle, moving through anarchy to oligarchy via tyranny, aristocracy, and monarchy. But it had come nowhere near any form of democracy—let alone polity—that Aristotle would have recognized. A bribed citizenship, removed from direct participation in their own rule, had turned into a mob. "To the City!" had been the cry of the crowds in 1844. By 1920, they were not only yelling, but dragging opponents from their cars and shooting them.

Lava Flow

By October 1922, the Greeks of Asia Minor were either dead, captive, or desperate to leave the crowded ports of a nation that didn't want them anymore. The volcano that erupted at Sakarya had released a lava flow of chaos and misery that fell hissing into the sea at Smyrna. The aftershocks were both swift and lasting. In Athens, after a series of coups and countercoups sponsored by rival factions of the army, the Second Hellenic Republic was set up. From the very start, its survival rested on the whim of a dangerously politicized army.

The 1923 Treaty of Lausanne took away everything Greece had gained three years earlier. Measured against Venizelos's grand ambitions, the new borders were a bitter disappointment. Compared to the tiny new kingdom of 1832, they were anything but. The new Greece was pretty much what it is today, and not so different from the territory of the classical Aegean city-states of the fifth century BCE.

Not Greater but Still Great

The Lausanne Treaty did not address the humanitarian crisis playing out on the seaboards of Greece and western Turkey. It was Venizelos who first proposed a population exchange. He could see that any return to the peaceful coexistence of centuries was unthinkable. And he glimpsed the possibility that something good might emerge from all the misery.

> ... a successful [population exchange] will enable us, within a few years, to recover from the heavy burdens which the war's unhappy outcome imposed on us—and to ensure, despite the collapse of Greater Greece, the consolidation of a Great Greece, whose borders will never be secure unless western Thrace and Macedonia are established as Greek territories, not only politically but ethnically.
>
> Venizelos to the Greek Foreign Ministry

In a letter to the nascent League of Nations, he requested that its first High Commissioner for Refugees, the Arctic explorer Fridtjof Nansen, be put in charge of the operation.

> We will request that this evacuation should be effected under the supervision of Dr. Nansen, who will certify that it has taken place in the most civilized way ... our moral standing in the civilized family of nations has been terribly diminished as a result of the arson and other acts of violence which the Greek army allowed itself to commit in Asia Minor.

Religion was to be the basis for the compulsory exchange of populations, the idea being that communities would be able to draw on deep bonds to make integration work. But there were many anomalies. Deep within Anatolia, whole villages were inhabited by Turkish-speaking Christians. In Crete there were Greek-speaking Muslims whose Christian ancestors had converted to Islam to avoid taxation under the Ottomans. Across much of the

Greek north were Greek-speaking Muslim majorities. All would be forced to leave their homes against their will.

The young Ernest Hemingway witnessed the horror of the Greek exodus from Eastern Thrace, henceforth part of Turkey:

> Twenty miles of carts drawn by cows, bullocks and muddy-flanked water buffalo, with exhausted, staggering men, women and children, blankets over their heads, walking blindingly along in the rain beside their worldly goods...

These people would repopulate the northern lands left by the departing Turks, who would themselves do the same in western Anatolia and on the Black Sea coast, where Greek communities had been living for nearly three millennia.

Venizelos knew very well that impoverished Greece was in no state to manage its part of the deal, and neither he nor Nansen had any qualms about appealing for outside help. The Americans

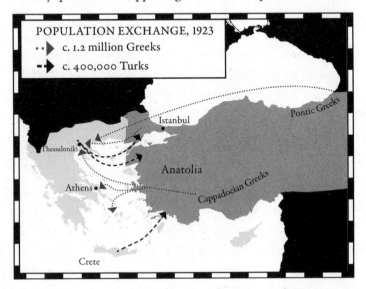

were first to respond, their Red Cross launching a $2.6 million relief effort, and others soon joined them.

Esther and Olga

America is great because she is good. If America ceases to be good, she will cease to be great.

Alexis de Tocqueville (1805–59)

Together with the Norwegian polymath Fridtjof Nansen, Esther Lovejoy embodied the international relief effort. As a doctor and founder of the American Women's Hospital Service (AWHS), she'd spent much of the war in France, helping civilian victims of the carnage. In 1922, she witnessed the horror that was unfolding in Greece and Turkey. Back in the US, she used radio broadcasts to spread the word and raise funds. She then returned to direct the work of the AWHS, whose all-female medical teams toiled in squalid conditions to save lives on the refugee-flooded Aegean islands.

On the islet of Macronisos, a quarantine station off the coast of Attica, things were so dire that the women were advised to leave. But Lovejoy's colleague, Olga Statsny from Omaha, was going nowhere. "My children are grown-up and married," she said, "I have no duties which could take precedence over my duties here." Olga stayed on the island for another five months and survived, while her Greek male assistant died of typhus.

Settlement

Soon more money was needed, and another American came forward to help: Henry Morgenthau, the former US ambassador to Constantinople. He'd seen for himself the suffering of migrants arriving at Thessaloniki.

> I saw seven thousand people crowded in a ship that would have been taxed to normal capacity with two thousand. They were packed like sardines upon the deck, a squirming, writhing mass of human misery.

The ambassador used his connections to tap the world's capital markets for a £10 million loan. So began the reconstruction of Greece under the auspices of the Refugee Settlement Commission. It would prove an outstanding success. By 1926, some 625,000 refugees had been provided with homes and become economically self-supporting.

The experience helps to explain Greek attitudes toward refugees today. In 2015, islanders in the eastern Mediterranean were confronted with hundreds of thousands of Muslim refugees seeking sanctuary on their shores. Many of those who volunteered assistance had grandparents who had first arrived on those islands from the hell of Smyrna, to be given help and hope. Now they were returning the kindness.

The population exchange triggered an inflow into Greece of around 1.4 million people, the proportional equivalent to eighty million making it over the border into the United States in one go. Naturally—the ancient tradition of *xenia* notwithstanding—there was prejudice on both sides. "Baptized in yogurt" was a common insult for the incomers, while educated Ottoman Greeks dismissed their supposedly primitive new compatriots as *palaioelladites* (old Greeks). The fear and mistrust would take decades to fade, but it was better than the alternative. Over one million Christian Armenians who'd had no choice but to remain in Turkey suffered one of the worst genocides in history.

As usually happens with immigration, Greece would be changed for the better. Almost all the Greeks of the Near East

Seeking sanctuary: refugee tents at the Temple of Hephaestus, Athens, in 1920

were now gathered within her borders, and this ethnic homogeneity would help the country escape future Balkan conflicts. Meanwhile the new arrivals brought with them an entrepreneurial vigor and know-how that would transform the economy.

According to the 1928 census, one in five of Greece's population were refugees. Their huge voting power—almost all were pro-Venizelos—could only deepen the National Schism. In 1923, they'd helped get rid of the monarchy. Four years later, in April 1927, they brought Venizelos back to power in the biggest electoral landslide in Greek history.

> [Venizelos] held in his hands the mandate to heal the split that he himself had played such a large part in creating.
> Roderick Beaton, *Greece: Biography of a Nation*

Would he grasp the opportunity?

Second Golden Age of Venizelism?

Not really. The four years after the *catastrophe* had been chaotic, as democratic interludes alternated with aggressive and populist military regimes rashly promising to reverse the humiliation of Lausanne. The elections of 1926—the first under proportional representation—had brought in what was called an "ecumenical" parliament that drew its members from both sides of the political divide. But the new majority system that Venizelos had engineered before his return meant that his 47 percent share of the vote became a 71 percent share of the seats in parliament. It also meant that he began his new term in office with half the population believing they'd been cheated.

Friendship Pact

Nevertheless, Venizelos forged ahead with reform. Land was redistributed, marshes reclaimed, and an embryonic welfare state set up. He also used his diplomatic flair to make new alliances—with Italy and Greece's erstwhile Balkan rivals—that reflected geopolitical realities. Astonishingly, he extended the hand of friendship to the biggest rival of them all. The Friendship Pact he signed with Turkey in October 1930 was a bold and genuinely statesmanlike move. He must have known that it would cost him support amongst his refugee voter base, since it formally renounced all claims against the Turkish state for the property they had lost during the *catastrophe*. Yet for Venizelos this was the price of finally fixing the borders. German Chancellor Hermann Müller described it as "the greatest achievement seen in Europe since the end of the Great War."

Meanwhile, the New York stock exchange had crashed. The Great Depression affected Greece less than other more developed European economies, but exports of tobacco, olive oil, and currants halved, and crucial remittances from the diaspora dried up. Venizelos threw economic liberalism to the wind. He took Greece off the gold standard and intervened directly to kick-start a recovery. None of it worked. In April 1932, Greece once again declared herself bankrupt. And Venizelos lost the next election.

THE END OF DEMOCRACY (1932–41)

Left-Right Divide

Not that the election of 1932 had any clear winners. The two main parties were almost evenly split, and incapable of consensus. A two-party debate on the best way to achieve the Great Idea had degraded into a republican-monarchist duel lethally turbocharged by an army that was itself deeply divided and had already intervened four times in Greece's short history as a nation. Greek democracy was starting to look like a Maniot feud. And for all his genius, Venizelos must take his share of the blame.

It was Venizelos who'd precipitated the National Schism by ignoring agreed-to neutrality during the First World War. He had used his "inexhaustible eloquence" to articulate an overambitious version of the Great Idea—both at home and abroad. The "ecumenical" parliament of 1926 had been a genuine attempt at unification, which Venizelos's majority system could only undermine. Aristotle must have been spinning in his grave.

As in the rest of Europe, Greek democracy now began to split into left-right camps. The truth was that Greek communists weren't much of a threat—Soviet insistence on an independent Macedonia fatally weakened their appeal—but Venizelos exaggerated the danger to bolster his support. Under his 1929 *idionym* law—enthusiastically adopted by later authoritarian regimes—anyone trying to "apply ideas that have as an obvious target the violent overthrow of the current social system" could be imprisoned. Over a thousand people were arrested and incarcerated under the law. Venizelos might have been the right man to steer the ship to new horizons, but it seemed he was the wrong one to be behind the wheel in a storm. The Second Hellenic Republic was a vessel without a compass, adrift on a rising sea.

When the 1933 elections brought back the royalists, a group of pro-Venizelos officers launched a coup. It failed, producing only an emergency military government. Violence escalated on the streets of Athens, and Venizelos's car was sprayed with bullets in an attempted assassination. In March 1935, he poured fuel on the flames, backing an insurrection across northern Greece and the islands. It was defeated, and the old man was condemned to death. He fled into exile in Paris. A year later, he was dead.

End of the Republic

A referendum held by the royalists showed a Soviet-style 98 percent of Greeks in favor of restoring the monarchy, and the Second Hellenic Republic quietly expired. In November 1935, King George II returned to try to impose order, but it was too late. The January elections saw the two feuding groups evenly split once again. This time, though, it was the Communist Party that held the balance of power.

Under the constitution, the king still had the right to appoint the prime minister. Now, egged on by the army, he was spooked into asking a soldier to form a government. General Metaxas led a party with just seven seats in parliament, and his appointment in August 1936 sparked mass unrest. Immediately he declared a state of emergency, dissolved parliament, and suspended civil liberties. So began the Fourth of August Regime, Greece's eccentric and not entirely convincing experiment in fascism.

Nazi salutes for Metaxas, the self-styled "First Peasant," in 1937

The Fourth of August Regime

Ioannis Metaxas was born into an aristocratic family in the Ionian islands and seems to have carried his fervent monarchism from the cradle. Trained at the Berlin War Academy, he'd fought in the Balkan Wars and entered the First World War as the army's deputy chief of staff, convinced that a Central Powers victory was inevitable. It was he who'd resigned over Venizelos's attempt to commit Greece to the Gallipoli campaign, which he (rightly) saw as too risky. He had also argued, almost alone, for restraint during the Anatolian Campaign in 1919–20.

Risk aversion and restraint were unusual qualities in a European fascist of the day. In other ways, too, Metaxas was not a model *führer*. Portly and bespectacled, he was more reminiscent of Colonel Klink than Mussolini. He was not racist, and in fact would repeal some of the anti-Semitic legislation of previous regimes.

He was, however, deeply hostile to Greece's chaotic brand of democracy. In his view, only a stable monarchy could hold back the "intemperate parliamentarianism" of men like Venizelos or the communist threat.

Backed by the army, the regime banned political parties, suborned the media, and outlawed industrial action. The minister for public order, Konstantinos Maniadakis, an altogether more convincing fascist and an admirer of Himmler, established a Greek version of the Gestapo (the *Asfaleia*), which rounded up all political opponents and subjected them to imprisonment, exile, and sometimes torture.

In other respects, the regime was more subtle—and contradictory. Ideologically, it reached back to both ancient Greece and Byzantium to find roots for its Third Hellenic Civilization. Yet the schools taught its history in demotic Greek rather than the *katharevousa* traditionally backed by the Right. The ghosts of Sparta were revived in the National Youth Organization (EON), where boys were instructed in self-discipline and girls primed to be dutiful mothers for new generations of virile Greeks. Economically, the regime sought to draw the sting of communism. The social security system set up by Venizelos was expanded, and workers were given shorter working weeks and maternity leave. Strikes were outlawed, but so were employers' lockouts.

In the royalist bastion of the Peloponnese, many liked the conservative values put forward by the "First Peasant," as Metaxas took to calling himself, sharing the Orthodox Church's view that he was a "blessing for Greece." In Athens, the Germanophile elite welcomed the injection of national discipline.

Fascist Rhodes

On the island of Rhodes, part of Italy since the Treaty of Lausanne, Greeks could observe at close quarters a more wholehearted version of fascism. An extraordinary new architecture had sprung up along the seafront—now with plenty of space for military parades—while in the bay, where once the Colossus had towered, a giant diving board rose from the sea as part of a new public beach where young Italians could show off their master-race athleticism. It's all still there today.

If there were other Greeks who struggled to take seriously the regime's silly uniforms and salutes, they didn't do much to challenge it. Anything seemed better than the endless cycle of violence that had come before. Besides, opposition could always be expressed in the back streets of Piraeus, where rowdy, illegal *rebetiko* gatherings attracted rich and poor alike.

Rebetiko band in Piraeus (1933). *Rebetiko* joined UNESCO's "Intangible Cultural Heritage" list in 2017.

Rebetiko

Rebetiko flowed in with refugees from the ports of the Anatolian seaboard. Like them, it was a flotsam of Greek, Turkish, and Middle Eastern influences. Its signature sound was the six-stringed, lute-like bouzouki and the smaller baglamas, which could be hidden down a trouser leg when the police came to call.

It quickly became the music of opposition, first among refugees then pretty much everyone else. As one Piraeus performer recalled with relish: "It was pandemonium every night... all sorts of people used to come. High-society aristocrats as well as *manges* [gangsters] and street kids and they'd rave it up until dawn."

> *Listen to the baglama playing,*
> *And find a joint for us.*
> *And when we get stoned,*
> *We have to be very careful.*
> *And when we get stoned,*
> *We have to be very careful.*
> *In case someone sees us,*
> *And they catch us,*
> *So they won't find a reason,*
> *And take us all to prison.*
> From *Otan Kapnizi o Loulas* ("When the Pipe Is Smoking")
> by Giorgos Mitsakis

Naturally this kind of thing was anathema to Metaxas & Co. It was unclean, un-Greek, and a recipe for disorder. The regime even went so far as to ban all phonograph records, just to be safe.

By the time of its comeback in the 1960s, *rebetiko* had moved out of the underworld to embrace themes lighter than lethal overdose or slit throats. The military junta in the 1970s did it the huge favor of banning it, instantly reinstating its protest credentials and its aura of the demimonde.

Ochi

Almost all Greeks agreed that the country should stay out of the war that Europe's other fascist regimes seemed so eager to start.

The general built a Metaxas Line along the Bulgarian border: a series of forts and other defenses that was supposed to keep invaders out. It was Greece's answer to the Maginot Line in France, and just as useless.

On April 4, 1939, Mussolini annexed Albania. A year and a half later, on the night of October 28, 1940, Metaxas woke to find the Italian ambassador, Emanuele Grazzi, standing at the foot of his bed to demand that Greece surrender key strategic sites or else face invasion. He answered in French, the language of diplomacy. "*Non*," he said ("ochi" in Greek).

The next day, October 29, Metaxas found himself suddenly a hero. Greeks still celebrate *Ochi* Day every year as a national holiday.

SECOND WORLD WAR (1941–45)

Swastika over the Parthenon

Mussolini's army duly rolled south out of Albania. If ever there was a time for Greeks to unite, it was now. And over the winter of 1940–41, when only Greece and the forces of the British Empire stood against the Axis powers, the nation came together as never before. Even ex-Venizelist officers rushed to enlist as ordinary soldiers. The world watched in amazement as the Italian army was stopped in its tracks, then driven back deep into Albania.

Britain provided limited air support, but Metaxas had declined Churchill's offer of troops. He was still desperate to keep his country out of the war and would do nothing to provoke Hitler. By January, dying of throat cancer, he knew his cause was lost: Germany would be forced to come to the aid of its useless ally because Hitler's invasion of Soviet Russia couldn't go ahead with its southern flank so exposed.

Britain was now asked to send reinforcements, but they were too little, and came too late. On April 6, the Germans crossed the

Bulgarian border. The British, Australian, and New Zealand troops were outflanked and forced to fall back into the Peloponnese (a young Roald Dahl taking to the skies in his Hurricane to help them), where a second Dunkirk took place at Kalamata.

The Germans sped on toward Athens, where the prime minister, Alexandros Koryzis, had already committed suicide in despair. Meanwhile, General Tsolakoglou, a divisional commander in the north, took it upon himself to surrender the entire Greek army to the Germans without first consulting his commander in chief. The king and his government fled to Crete, only to be ejected once again a month later when German airborne troops seized the island. The government would spend the rest of the war in exile in Cairo.

Second Panzer Division troops raise the swastika over the Acropolis, April 1941.

On April 27, 1941, the swastika was raised over the Parthenon. Few images better capture the triumph of tyranny over democracy, yet this was a victory Hitler had never anticipated. He had no quarrel with Greece. It was only *il Duce*'s ineptitude that had brought him there.

> I perhaps better than anyone can share your feelings with regard to a place where all that we today call human culture found its beginning.
>
> Letter from Hitler to Mussolini, 1942

Starvation

Whatever the *Führer*'s personal feelings, his intervention was short and ruthless. The Germans systematically stripped Greece of her means of survival, before most marched back to rejoin Operation Barbarossa. A few strategically important sites remained under their control—parts of Athens, Thessaloniki, and territory near the border with Turkey—while almost everything else was handed over to Mussolini, whom the Greeks considered they had already defeated. The exceptions were eastern Macedonia and western Thrace, where the Bulgarian occupiers set in motion a vicious program of ethnic cleansing.

With the country looted and the fertile plains of Macedonia and Thrace lost, Greeks now faced winter famine on a colossal scale. The task of distributing what little food remained fell to Tsolakoglou and his quisling government, but his cabinet of generals was as incompetent as it was unpopular.

No one knows exactly how many Greeks died over the terrible winter of 1941–42, but the figure of two hundred thousand in Athens alone is widely accepted. Famine brought with it disease, as the dead lay unburied in the streets. The abandoned royal estate at Tatoi in the foothills of Mt. Parnitha outside Athens was stripped of its trees and grass for fuel and food. The rich joined the poor in the breadlines.

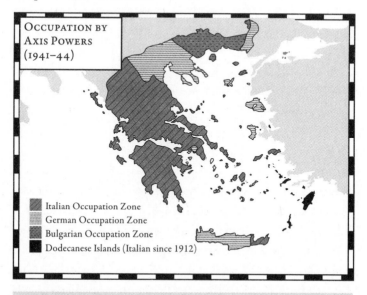

OCCUPATION BY
AXIS POWERS
(1941–44)

Italian Occupation Zone
German Occupation Zone
Bulgarian Occupation Zone
Dodecanese Islands (Italian since 1912)

SS *Kurtulus*

In the 1930s, Venizelos had held out an olive branch to Turkey. This move probably cost him the 1932 election, but without it one of the most extraordinary episodes of the war might never have happened.

In October 1941, as famine gripped Athens, a Turkish ship slipped out of Istanbul laden with grain. She was the *SS Kurtulus* ("Liberation") and she'd been hired by the Turkish government to carry aid to its old enemy under the banner of the Red Crescent.

On her fifth humanitarian voyage, in February 1942, the *Kurtulus* sank in the Sea of Marmara during a storm, but the Turks continued to send aid to Greece until 1946. One of their ships even brought a thousand half-starved and traumatized Greek children back to safety in Istanbul.

Greeks and Turks are supposed to be enemies, but they can also be good neighbors. When an earthquake struck the Turkish town of Izmit in 1999, Greeks were first on the scene to help. And when Athens suffered a similar disaster a few months later, the Turks were first there too.

The occupying powers did their best to make things worse. They began to charge Greece for the costs of occupation—costs that could only be met by printing more money. Inflation, then hyperinflation, took the price of a loaf of bread from seventy to two million drachma as the middle classes saw their savings evaporate. With the government utterly unable to cope, the black market seeped into every corner of the economy. On the islands things were little better. Boats were requisitioned, fishing forbidden, and inter-island trade banned.

The Italians begged for German help, but were told to work it out themselves.

The Germans have taken from the Greeks even their shoelaces, and they now pretend to place the blame for the economic situation on our shoulders.

Mussolini

Resistance

At first resistance was scattered and spontaneous. British POWs were cheered as they were driven through Athens. Graffiti was daubed on walls. Most dramatically, the swastika above the Acropolis was torn down and replaced with the Greek flag.

Over time, sporadic protests gave way to a more planned and organized resistance. With the king in exile and the government in Athens collaborating with the occupiers, the Greek Communist Party (KKE) filled the leadership vacuum. In October 1941, it formed the National Liberation Front (EAM) and soon afterward its military wing, ELAS. Young activists fanned out from Athens into the rest of the country to organize the food, education, and administration that the government had failed to provide.

EAM membership grew quickly, and by 1944 had reached about two million. Its message had changed from class struggle to national liberation (the acronym ELAS is just one *L* short of the *katharevousa* word for Greece, *Ellas*), and was aimed to attract everyone who wanted to resist occupation, then build a fairer postwar nation. It was disingenuous, as we shall see, but it suited the needs of the time.

Greek Women at War

In a rigidly patriarchal society, women were especially drawn to EAM's message of equality.

Since ancient times, Greek women had played a crucial role in military success. Plutarch claimed that a Spartan wife, when handing her husband his shield as he marched off to battle, told him to come back either with it or on it (i.e., dead). In the War of Independence, admirals like the hard-drinking Bouboulina of Spetses fought and sailed with skill and success, while a group of Maniot military wives famously sent the Egyptians scrambling back to their boats when they tried to land on the beach at Diros.

But it was in the Greek Civil War of the 1940s that women fought side by side with men for the first time, sharing the same hardships, the same dangers, often the same sleeping bags. When ELAS partisans took to the streets in Athens in 1944, a women's battalion marched down Andrea Syngrou Avenue shouting, "Down with virginity!"

Interventions

Meanwhile Greece had become more strategically important. Hitler was convinced the Allies planned to attack from North Africa, and Churchill did what he could to bolster that belief by encouraging partisan activity. But he found ELAS less palatable than the smaller, noncommunist EDES, whose leaders were only too happy to paint their rival as a Trojan horse for a communist takeover of Europe. When the two partisan groups turned on each other in October 1943, Churchill cut off all support to ELAS, even though it was by far the largest and most effective arm of the Greek resistance.

Outside Greece, the tide of the war was changing, and bit by bit the good news seeped in. In February 1943, the Germans were defeated at Stalingrad, and in May, in North Africa, too. In July, Mussolini was ejected, and the Italians surrendered. In Greece, ninety thousand Italian soldiers, thoroughly fed up with Greek stubbornness and the ridicule of their German allies, laid down their arms. By autumn, most of the weapons were in the hands of ELAS.

Democracy in War

The image of the swastika flying over the Acropolis may have looked like a symbol of the triumph of fascism over democracy, but the state the Nazis took over had little in common with the political system that had built the Parthenon.

Ironically, Greece's wartime occupation helped revive this more ancient notion of democracy, if only for a short time. The EAM and ELAS leadership were no democrats, yet the administrations they set up in towns and villages across Greece had elements of the direct democracy of the *poleis* two and a half millennia before.

> The benefits of civilisation and culture trickled into the mountains for the first time. Schools, local government, law courts and public utilities, which the war had ended, worked again. Theatres, factories, parliamentary assemblies began for the first time.

C. M. Woodhouse, head of the Allied Military Mission to Greece

After the war, Manolis Glezos, the nineteen-year-old boy who'd torn down the swastika from the Acropolis and joined the *andartes* (partisans) in the mountains, remembered what had been achieved. He resigned his seat in parliament to set up an experiment in direct democracy in the village of Aperanthou on his native Naxos. He penned a constitution,

formed an assembly, and invited the community to participate in all areas of local government. It didn't last, but it held
up a mirror to the dysfunctional, polarized Greek politics of
the time.

Total War Comes to Greece

The euphoria was short-lived. Hitler replaced the Italians with
troops transferred from the collapsing eastern front. These men,
brutalized by their experiences fighting the Russians, brought
with them a different kind of warfare.

All armed men are basically to be shot on the spot. Villages
from where shots have been fired, or where armed men have
been encountered, are to be destroyed.

Instructions given to the 1st Mountain Division in Greece

Fifty Greeks were to die for every German soldier killed, ten for
every wounded German, with no distinction made between guilty
and innocent. A concentration camp appeared outside Athens,
run by a drunk named Radomski. His year-long reign of brutality
was too much even for the SS, who dismissed him for the crime
of threatening to shoot his own adjutant. "A very primitive man,"
was the verdict of the tribunal.

By early 1944, anti-guerrilla sweeps by the Germans had left
corpses hanging from trees, and villages without villagers. At
Komeno, Kalvryta, and Distomo, there were wholesale massacres.
In the end, it was as self-defeating as it had been when Ibrahim
Pasha had ravaged the Peloponnese more than a century earlier.
Now as then, the Greeks left their burning villages and joined the
andartes in the mountains.

Women and men fought alongside each other in the partisan groups run by ELAS.

Genocide in Thessaloniki

The Jewish community accounted for about a third of the population of Greece's second city. At first the occupiers confined themselves to seizing property and acts of humiliation. On the "Black Sabbath" of Saturday, July 11, 1942, all Jewish men were ordered to gather at Eleftheria Square, where they were exercised en masse for the entertainment of visiting dignitaries, until they dropped from exhaustion.

In February 1943, Dieter Wisliceny, an expert in the business of death, arrived in the city. Deportations to Auschwitz began almost immediately, and by the start of June, some fifty thousand men, women, and children—the city's entire Jewish population—had ridden the cattle trucks north. Auschwitz's records show that of the 48,974 Greek Jews who arrived in the camp, 37,387 went straight into the gas chambers.

Mother of Israel

Perhaps 90 percent of Greece's Jewish population were killed in the "Final Solution," one of the highest proportions in Europe. The majority were Sephardic Jews from Thessaloniki, where they'd lived since their expulsion from Spain in 1492, speaking a fusion of medieval Spanish and Hebrew called Ladino. The city soon acquired the nickname *Madre de Israel*, thanks to the brilliant reputation of its Jewish scholars.

The Jews of Thessaloniki created enormous wealth for the city. One speciality was spinning wool, using techniques brought over from Spain. The warm, waterproof cloth was of such high quality that in the sixteenth century Sultan Selim II decreed that it must be worn by his Janissary regiments. But as the orders rose, so the quality fell, until the Chief Rabbi was summoned to Istanbul and executed.

End in Sight

By April 1944, it had become clear to the Germans that they needed the help of the Greek-manned Security Battalions. They were now unleashed on their civilian compatriots to terrorize them into obedience. It didn't work. By the time the Germans finally pulled out six months later, in October 1944, EAM/ELAS was firmly in charge across free Greece (everywhere outside the big cities), and its politics were hardening. The rhetoric became more Soviet and the reprisals more savage. *Andartes* courts meted out harsh punishment to "reactionaries" while assassination squads disposed of "enemies of the people" without waiting for the courts.

But the communists were about to lose their main sponsors. After a vodka-fueled dinner in Moscow in October 1944, Stalin and Churchill scribbled their infamous Percentages Agreement on the back of a Russian napkin. It sketched the parceling-out of Eastern Europe after the war: Yugoslavia and Hungary to be split evenly; Romania 90 percent Russian; Greece 90 percent Western. Soon afterward, a Soviet delegation broke the bad news to the EAM leadership.

With Stalin's support in doubt, EAM was forced to compromise. The excesses of the Security Battalions had driven many into its ranks who were far from communist. Now they just wanted peace. The leadership agreed to place its forces under British command and join a new government of national unity, though sixty thousand partisans were still under arms. It seemed little had changed since the departure of the Bavarians a century before. The Great Powers were still calling the shots.

Battle for Athens

In Athens, however, there was little appetite for dealing with the official government, now back from its Cairo exile. It was in the capital that the Security Battalions had committed their worst atrocities—with the king's blessing, it was widely believed.

Greek Security Battalions

The Security Battalions were set up by the quisling government in 1943. Not trusted at first by the Germans, they were poorly armed and manned by an uneasy coalition of Nazi sympathizers and moderates who feared the communists' postwar intentions.

Things changed with the windfall of Italian arms to ELAS and the return of Germans bent on total war. The Battalions quickly grew into a well-armed German auxiliary force under the command of the SS. Their mission was to cow the population into withdrawing all support for the *andartes*. The men were often told that their murders and rapes would be pardoned even if the Allies won the war, because the king and the British were secretly on their side.

In the summer of 1944, the Battalions sealed off entire districts of Athens and lined up citizens in front of informers wearing hoods, who picked out alleged EAM members for execution.

Now that the war in Greece was over, Athenians saw these collaborators not only going unpunished, but being actively recruited into the new National Guard. Unsurprisingly, the partisans halted their demobilization, and the two EAM ministers appointed to the new government resigned. Three days later, mass protests erupted across

All to Arms! All to the Barricades!
EAM poster from December 1944

Athens. In Constitution Square, the police panicked and fired into the crowd. Ten were killed and fifty wounded, sparking a general uprising.

Churchill sent in British troops to restore order. ELAS turned on them and a full-scale battle broke out in the streets of Athens. British reinforcements were rushed in from Italy. Now badly outgunned, most partisans took to the mountains, and it was all over in a month. To the consternation of his advisers, Churchill risked flying to Athens on Christmas Day to see the situation for himself. Finally accepting how unpopular the king was, he persuaded him to stay in Cairo until a plebiscite decided the future of the Greek monarchy.

Tanks and troops of the 5th (Scots) Parachute Battalion pursuing ELAS on the streets of Athens, December 18, 1944

The December Events, as the battle for Athens is known in Greece, were over, but the mood remained dangerously volatile. With British troops ensuring no ELAS comeback, Greek anti-communists began to round up communist sympathizers. In February 1945, a treaty was signed at Varkiza that promised to include EAM in the political process if they agreed to lay down arms. Yet the White Terror continued unabated. Government forces hunted down, tortured, and deported (often to British camps in the Middle East) anyone suspected of pro-communist views. The country was sliding inexorably back toward civil war.

Was Churchill to blame?

The December events opened a well of bitterness toward Britain that has not run dry. Many Greeks believe that Churchill actively thwarted the will of the Greek people after the war, backing an unpopular and ineffectual king who had spent the occupation years in exile, and dismissing the partisans who had risked their lives fighting the Germans as nothing more than "miserable banditti."

Perhaps Churchill's obsession with communism blinded him to the fact that Greece was a country of smallholders who believed fervently in property ownership. Most of the villagers who joined ELAS were as obstinate as their *klepht* forefathers— obstinate, but not communist. Without Soviet muscle behind it, communism would likely not have taken root in Greece. Arguably, Churchill's intervention helped trigger the devastating civil war that would shatter all hope of postwar unity.

If the Greeks hadn't fought…

The Second World War was a calamity for Greece. Perhaps one in fifteen Greeks died from fighting, famine, reprisals, or in the camps. Over a million were left without homes. In Epirus, according to the Red Cross, 40 percent of the rural population was "in immediate danger of extinction." Greece had endured national suffering on a staggering scale. Yet Hitler had only come to Greece to clean up after his ally. Had all this suffering served any purpose?

Perhaps if the Germans hadn't been sidetracked by events in Greece, they would have launched the invasion of Russia a month earlier, and they might well have reached Moscow. In December 1941, the *Wehrmacht*'s advance units were only thirteen miles short of the Russian capital when the fuel froze in their tanks.

Hitler himself would later blame the Balkan campaign for the disaster of Operation Barbarossa. And many would say that Hitler's failure to conquer Russia cost him the entire war.

Civil War

When General Plastiras took over as prime minister in January 1945, it was correctly seen by Greeks as a choice made in London. It was not a wise appointment. Britain wanted to stabilize Greece, then leave, but the general, though a hero of the Turkish campaign of the 1920s, was not the man to promote stability. He was loathed by EAM for his wartime leadership of EDES, and he was loathed by the royalists as an arch-republican. His three months in office only heightened tensions. A succession of unhappy leaders came after him, before elections were set for March 1946. They were the first in ten years.

With the Right more and more confident—and armed—Britain saw little risk in flying Nikos Zachariadis, erstwhile secretary-general of the Communist Party, back from Germany, where he'd spent the war in a concentration camp. But Zachariadis chose to boycott the elections, arguing with some justification that they couldn't be fair in the current climate. The predictable result was a massive victory for the Right. Another rigged referendum on the monarchy followed, with a 70-30 split supposedly in favor of the king's return.

For the Left, armed struggle now seemed the only option. The communist governments of Albania, Bulgaria, and Yugoslavia pledged support, and several thousand Greek comrades moved over the border to undergo military training in the camps that had been set up there. Having just emerged from one terrible war, the country now plunged headlong into another.

Stylianos Kyriakides

During the Greek Civil War, the patriotism that had brought Greeks together during the occupation would curdle into divisions and hatreds that are still felt today. The story of Stylianos Kyriakides helps to show what was lost.

Kyriakides was born to a poor family in a mountain village in Cyprus. The youngest of five children, he left home at sixteen to become the houseboy of a British medical officer, himself an amateur athlete, who taught him to run. At the Pan-Cyprian Games in 1932, Stylianos won the 1,500 and 10,000 meters on Friday, then the 5,000 and 20,000 meters on Sunday. He competed for Greece in Hitler's 1936 Berlin Olympics, before returning home to fight him, and was once spared summary execution when a German soldier saw his pass from the Berlin Games.

In 1946, Kyriakides sold his possessions to buy the airfare to travel to Boston to take part in the city's marathon. As the race neared its climax, he was in third place when an old man cried out from the crowd: "Do it for Greece! For your children!" Stylianos lifted his head and began to pull away. Moments later, he crossed the finish line first, shouting as he did so: "For Greece!"

Kyriakides, wearing his victory laurels: a Greek hero

How can you beat a guy like that? He wasn't running for himself, he was doing it for his country.

Johnny Kelley, the American defending champion

Kyriakides used his new celebrity to ask the Americans for help in easing the hardships of his fellow Greeks. He came home with twenty-five tons of American aid and $250,000 ($3.5 million now) in cash. More than a million people gathered from all over Greece to cheer him through the streets of Athens. At the ceremony at the Temple of Zeus, he uttered these simple words: "I am proud to be Greek."

Truman Doctrine

The civil war started—or restarted—in late 1946 with a full-scale communist offensive from the north. At first it looked like the communists might achieve a quick victory, not least because Britain, now under a Labour government, had set a date of March 1947 for the withdrawal of its troops. But just three weeks before that deadline, President Truman announced his famous doctrine, which guaranteed American help to any state threatened by communist takeover. Almost immediately, arms and money flooded into Greece.

Gradually, and with Stalin staying aloof, the war went the government's way, though not as fast as America wanted, since the communists could always find sanctuary in neighboring communist states. But when, in 1948, Tito fell out with Stalin and Yugoslavia was thrown out of the Soviet-led eastern bloc alliance, Cominform, the KKE chose loyalty to Moscow over support from its neighbors. In July 1949, Yugoslavia closed its border and disbanded the KKE camps. By the end of September, the civil war was all over.

Aftermath

The killing had stopped, but the horror lingered. Nine years of fighting had left half a million people dead and another seven hundred thousand—a staggering 10 percent of the population—homeless. The country was traumatized by atrocities committed by both sides, and the violence that had torn communities apart. Spain still feels the wounds of a civil war that ended about eighty years ago, and America still reels from the one that finished seventy years before that. Like those conflicts, the Greek Civil War had pitched friend against friend, husband against wife, sibling against sibling, Greek against Greek. Its aftereffects would be no less lasting.

PART FOUR

Democracy Debased
1949–PRESENT

THE AMERICAN AGE (1947–74)

Client State

The years after the civil war saw astonishing, America-backed economic growth. Between 1945 and 1950, Greece received over $2 billion in US aid, much of it through the Marshall Plan. The results were spectacular. Between the mid-1950s and late 1970s, GDP grew nearly 7 percent a year and per capita income tripled. It wasn't far short of the German postwar miracle.

Greece gained the Dodecanese islands from Italy in 1947, reaching the borders she has today, and islands like Rhodes helped to fuel the boom in tourism that began in the 1950s. And yet in the three decades from 1951 to 1980, about a million Greeks—a quarter of the active workforce—chose to emigrate. How much of this was due to the effects of the civil war can only be guessed at.

The price of American largesse was that Greece effectively became a client state. Great Power interference was nothing new, but now every important political decision had to be sanctioned by Washington. Old hands at gaming their own democracy, the Americans insisted on a majority voting system in Greece, ensuring a decade of parliamentary dominance for the Right. State jobs were dished out according to political criteria, and if you were on the Left you might as well not apply. Thousands of former partisans were imprisoned on remote Greek islands.

Macronisos

Seen from the sky, the islet of Macronisos, just off the coast of Attica, looks like a spearhead, as black and hard as the obsidian blades once traded there. By the time the first political prisoners arrived after the civil war, it was a place long used to misery and death. During the camp's construction, hundreds of Turkish graves were discovered, dating back to the Balkan

Postwar prison camp on Macronisos

wars of the early twentieth century when the island was used as a POW camp.

In 1922, Macronisos was repurposed as a quarantine station for incoming refugees from Anatolia. It was the place from where Olga Statsny of Omaha had refused to budge when disease was laying waste to all around her. In postwar Greece, it was prison to thousands whose political convictions did not suit the state. They included Apostolos Santas, one of the two young men who had climbed the Acropolis to tear down the Nazi flag.

Many other dissidents went into exile in Tashkent, capital of Uzbekistan. There they joined Greeks who'd been forcibly resettled by Stalin from other parts of the USSR, and others still who'd been there for so many centuries that they barely even knew they were Greek.

Resentment at American interference during this period tended to focus on the monarchy, seen as stooges of Uncle Sam. King Paul, who came to the throne in 1947 after the death of his elder brother George, made no secret of his right-wing sympathies, and nor did his queen, Frederica of Hanover. Their interference in politics helped create a swell of republicanism across the country.

Postwar Greece was very far from being a liberal paradise, but neither was it Stalinist Russia. Censorship was mild and there was little outright brutality. By 1952, many prisoners had been released from the Aegean camps and many exiles had returned home. During Konstantinos Karamanlis's first term as prime minister from 1955 to 1963, a program of rapid industrialization, heavy investment in infrastructure, agriculture, and tourism was driven through. Women were finally given full voting rights in the election of 1956.

As during the Third Hellenic Republic of the 1930s, dissent tended to be expressed in the cultural realm. The composer Mikis Theodorakis set the communist poetry of Giannis Ritsos to his sublime and distinctly Greek music. The film star Melina Mercouri won international fame by playing a new kind of Greek woman, as independent and full of *philotimo* as her brothers. Popular culture rather than politics was shaping attitudes, and in contrast to some other European countries, that culture wasn't enslaved to Hollywood.

Mercouri in the 1960 hit movie *Never on Sunday*

Cyprus

Cyprus had been a British colony since 1878 and its population was split 80 percent Greek, 20 percent Turkish. For as long as anyone could remember, a majority of the island's Greeks had been pushing for *enosis*. They had been thwarted first by British reluctance to lose a colonial possession, then by the American desire to maintain NATO's southern flank, which depended on Turkish cooperation.

In 1955, a new, more violent campaign for union with Greece erupted, with the quiet encouragement of the island's leader, Archbishop Makarios. Britain refused to discuss the possibility, and even went so far as to lure Turkey into the debate as a counterweight to Greece. It was a mistake. In September 1955, violence broke out in Istanbul, sparking a mass exodus of almost all remaining Greeks from Turkey. Soon the Turks were matching the Greek call for *enosis* with their own demand for partition.

In 1959, Britain brokered a deal by which Cyprus would become independent, despite serious misgivings by Makarios, who correctly saw that the new constitution was too pro-Turk and so not fit for purpose. It wasn't long before the new power-sharing arrangements collapsed and UN troops arrived to keep the peace. They're still there today.

The Old Fool and the Young Rascal

After two decades of right-wing rule, popular dissent finally surfaced in the political sphere. Georgios Papandreou founded the new Center Union party, a coalition of old Venizelists, liberals, and dissatisfied conservatives. He declared a "relentless struggle" against the *parakratos* (deep state) of the Right, with the unseating of Karamanlis as its top priority.

Papandreou caught the popular mood. Greeks wanted an end to what seemed like one-party rule, as well as to foreign interference and a monarchy whose political leanings were all too clear. Some of his rhetoric could have come straight from the lips of the French revolutionary leader Georges Danton:

> They have called this the noise of a mob. I say it is the voice of the Greek people. Let them hear it in the palace!
>
> Georgios Papandreou

After the 1964 election, he became prime minister with a landslide victory. But though he was to the left of Karamanlis, he was no revolutionary. Staunchly anti-communist and pro-NATO, his economic and labor reforms were mild. He and the new king, Constantine II, might have detested each other, but he made no move to abolish the monarchy.

His son, Andreas, now finance minister, was a different matter. Charismatic and with a gift for populist speechifying, he was a worry to the Americans, whose Marine Corps was about to land on Vietnam's China Beach. "The old fool and the young rascal" was how Secretary of State Dean Acheson referred to the two Papandreous.

In 1965, a somewhat obscure sequence of events known as the *Aspida* Plot resulted in Georgios Papandreou's resignation.

The Aspida *Plot*

Aspida means "shield" in Greek.* In 1965, it was the code name for a secret organization of junior officers sworn to resist a

---

* It's the word Ursula von der Leyen, president of the European Commission, recently used while visiting the migrant camps of the Aegean, to describe the part assigned to Greece in the refugee crisis.

right-wing takeover of the army, an ever-present threat in 1960s Greece. Rumors—probably untrue, possibly fanned by the Americans—of Andreas Papandreou's involvement began to circulate. The defense minister announced an inquiry into the scandal but was forced to resign in the face of outrage from Papandreou father and son. Georgios announced that he would take over the Ministry of Defense himself, but this was vetoed by the king. After an explosive meeting, the prime minister submitted his resignation.

Athenians took to the streets. The ex–prime minister was now determined to fan the spreading republican flame. "The king reigns," he yelled into the crowds, "but the people rule." Amid mounting strikes and protests, the king set up a string of interim administrations, none of which lasted long. Finally, new elections were set for May 1967. They never happened.

The Marx Brothers without the Talent

The CIA was—and still is—widely believed to have been behind the army coup that took place on the night of Friday, April 21, 1967. After all, as cynical Athenians quipped, nothing so efficient could possibly have happened without American involvement.

It was certainly efficient. The city woke up to find tanks in strategic positions throughout the city, including parliament, the palace, and the national television center, and army units arresting anyone suspected of leftist sympathies. Georgios Papandreou was rousted from his bed and held at bayonet point, while Andreas escaped onto the roof of his villa, only to give himself up when a soldier captured his small son and held a gun to his head.

The Americans probably knew no more about it than the Greek army chief, who was among those arrested. This was a coup staged by a mediocre trio of two colonels and a brigadier, aptly characterized by the travel writer Peter Levi as "the Marx Brothers without the talent." From the start, they were pariahs.

Two Colonels and a Brigadier: the Greek junta in 1967

The king played it wrong at every turn. Unlike his brother-in-law, Juan Carlos, fourteen years later in Spain, Constantine made no attempt to rally the country to resist. Instead, he swore in the new government, albeit reluctantly, and so gave it some of the legitimacy it desperately needed.

We don't know how much pressure the Americans put on Constantine. We do know that they quickly recovered from their surprise and moored an aircraft carrier off the coast to show their support for the coup. And we know that they turned a blind eye—as did the British government under Harold Wilson—to the regime's later use of torture, often carried out by prison officials who'd served under the Nazi occupation. The Colonels, as the military junta came to be known, may have been sons of bitches, but to echo President Roosevelt's verdict on a Nicaraguan dictator of the 1930s, they were "America's sons of bitches."

The new regime started in familiar style. Martial law was proclaimed, political parties banned, parliament closed, and opponents arrested—the composer Theodorakis again among them. The actress Melina Mercouri had her Greek citizenship revoked.

I was born a Greek and will die a Greek. Those bastards were born fascists and will die fascists.

Melina Mercouri

At first, the king tried to work with the new regime, but once their ineptitude became clear, he attempted a countercoup. It failed, and he fled to Britain.

A Patient in Need of Surgery

Life under the junta—as the new regime was soon dubbed, with the contempt generally aimed at rulers of Latin American banana republics—was restrictive, sometimes violent, and often bizarre. Colonel George Papadopoulos, its front man, might like to talk grandly about the "Revolution of April 21" but in fact his regime was little more than a parade of phobias: xenophobia, homophobia, ephebiphobia.*

Papadopoulos and his cronies saw Greece as a patient in need of surgery. Her illness was caused by an overdose of consumerism, and the cure was the enforcement of strict Orthodox Christian values. Churchgoing and traditional folk music were in; long hair and miniskirts (except the ones worn by the National Guard) were out. Elections could only be brought back once the medicine had taken effect.

Along with communists, undesirable foreigners were sent packing, including the painter John Craxton, who had been living on Crete. Craxton was the human synthesis of the Colonels' numerous phobias: a gay artist who didn't bother to hide his contempt for the regime and whose predilection for military personnel led some to suspect him of espionage.

The junta lasted as long as it did largely thanks to the still booming economy, but the twenty thousand secret informers at work on the streets of Athens also played a part. Yet despite the fear they inspired, there was opposition. As so often in Greece, it came from the artists.

* "Fear of youth," from the Greek *ephebe*.

Giorgos Seferis

Greeks have always revered their poets. Among the moderns, Giorgos Seferis (1900–71) and the Alexandrian Constantine Cavafy (1863–1933) are perhaps the best loved. Seferis's family were refugees from Smyrna, and a strong sense of exile and loss runs through his poetry. After studying law in Paris, he joined the Foreign Service, and from 1957 to 1961 was Greek ambassador in London. In March 1969, back in Greece, he made a statement to the BBC, distributing copies of it to every newspaper in Athens:

> All those intellectual values that we succeeded in keeping alive, with agony and labour, are about to sink into the abyss . . . I am a man without any political affiliation, and I can therefore speak without fear or passion. I see ahead of me the precipice toward which the oppression that has shrouded the country is leading us. This anomaly must stop. It is a national imperative.

Seferis broadcasting at the BBC the 1950s

Two years later he was dead, some say of a broken heart. Up to his last days, Athenians would cross the street to shake his hand. At his funeral in Athens, vast crowds, old and young, followed his coffin through the streets, singing his poem "Denial" (which had been banned by the regime) set to the music of Mikis Theodorakis. At his graveside, his widow, Maro, cut off her hair and threw it in.

The opening ceremony of the 2004 Olympic Games began with the poetry of Seferis. As the national anthem died away, seventy-two thousand spectators—among them fifty heads of state—fell silent as the famous stanza from "Mythistorema" was read:

I woke with this marble head in my hands;

it exhausts my elbow and I don't know where to put it down.

It was falling into the dream as I was coming out of the dream

so our life became one and it will be very difficult for it to separate again.

The outpouring of rage at Seferis's funeral failed to unseat the junta, but time was running out for the Colonels.

Bread! Education! Liberty!

The 1973 oil crisis shook the Greeks out of their apathy. Twenty years of uninterrupted economic growth ground to a halt as inflation hit double digits. The Greeks looked at each other, then at the Marx Brothers who ruled them. Things had to change.

The students moved first. In November they massed at the Athens Polytechnic, chanting "Bread! Education! Liberty!" and broadcasting events live to the world via a homemade transmitter. Within three days, as many as a hundred thousand protesters had gathered, and running battles were being fought with the police. This was too much for the Colonels. They sent in the tanks. The first smashed through the Polytechnic gates, crushing the legs of a girl. The student radio called out for doctors, then fell silent. Army marines were inside the campus with fixed bayonets, beating up students too slow to escape.

Uprising at the Athens Polytechnic. *Bread! Education! Liberty!*

Campus Asylum

November 17 ("*Polytechneio*") is still a school holiday in Greece, when the country's leaders lay wreaths for the twenty-four students who died during the protests and the many more who were imprisoned and tortured under the Colonels. The crowds march from there to the American embassy, a sign of how many Greeks still see the CIA as complicit.

After the junta, a law was passed to ban all police or military presence on university campuses. For decades after the tanks plowed through the student barriers in 1973, Greeks lived with its perverse consequences: chaos within Greece's higher education system, with universities in central Athens regularly closed by anarchist student sit-ins, and others turning into open yet untouchable marketplaces for drugs and other contraband.

In 2019, Prime Minister Mitsotakis abolished the Asylum Law, and (almost) everyone in Greece raised a glass of ouzo.

The End of the Junta

The brutality with which the junta had treated the students hardened the mood of the Greek people. Now loathed by every section of society, the regime doubled down. Papadopoulos was removed and the even more hard-line Brigadier Dimitrios Ioannidis took his place. He knew that only a miracle could keep him there, and his gaze turned to Cyprus, where Greeks and Turks were shooting each other in the streets. Perhaps by toppling the Cypriot government and forcing *enosis* with the motherland he could cling to power? So it was that Archbishop Makarios awoke to find Greek tanks on his lawn. Then the Turks invaded.

After thousands had died, hundreds of thousands had been displaced from their homes, and two members of NATO had very nearly gone to war, the Americans brokered a peace that divided the island between Greek and Turk, as it remains today.

The Colonels' time was up. Senior politicians and army generals called on Karamanlis to return in order to oversee the dismantlement of the junta and a return to democracy. No serious threat has come from the army ever since.

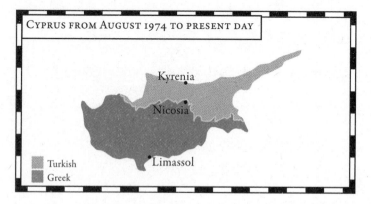

CYPRUS FROM AUGUST 1974 TO PRESENT DAY

Kyrenia

Nicosia

Limassol

Turkish
Greek

The West Means Europe

Since his defeat in the 1963 elections to Georgios Papandreou, Karamanlis had been living in Paris. On the night of July 24, 1974, he touched down in Athens, determined to bring about the change that the Greek people demanded. His New Democracy party had done America's bidding right up to the coup, but now he'd reach back to Aristotle's "Golden Mean," or moderation between extremes, to find consensus. Over the next six years, he got rid of the monarchy (after a referendum in which 69 percent voted to do so), legalized the Communist Party, released all political prisoners, and brought the perpetrators of the junta to justice.

As for the America question, henceforth the West would mean Europe. Karamanlis renewed negotiations to join the European Economic Community (EEC) as a full member, and in 1981 Greece was accepted amid rhetoric that echoed the philhellenic fervor of 1821:

> [Greek entry into the EEC] is a fitting repayment by the Europe of today of the cultural and political debt that we all owe to a Greek heritage almost 3,000 years old.
>
> EEC junior Foreign Office minister, 1980

Perhaps Karamanlis's most popular move was the final abolition of *katharevousa*. Demotic was brought in as the official language of education, and Greek officialese at last became comprehensible to everyone.

Katharevousa

Katharevousa was invented by Adamantios Korais. Its aim was to purify the Greek that had evolved over the two millennia since the end of the classical era into something closer to the ancient version. First, a written language with ancient roots would be created; over time this would transform the spoken tongue; and from there, eventually, the minds and morals of its speakers.

> The hearts and minds of the modern Greeks will be elevated by writing ancient Greek . . . they will thereby learn Truth and Freedom.
>
> Panagiotis Soutsos, 1853

It was wishful thinking. Without the unifying political culture of ancient Greece, the new hybrid language could as easily divide as empower. If the politicians wanted to keep the people far from the reins of power, *katharevousa* was certainly helping their cause.

> The pedants are speaking and writing in a language the nation doesn't understand.
>
> Andreas Laskaratos (1811–1901), poet

By the 1890s, many poets and novelists were writing in demotic. Things came to a head in the aftermath of the Greek-Turkish War of 1897, when Queen Olga unwittingly poured fuel on the fire. While reading passages from the Bible to wounded Greek soldiers in hospital, she was struck by how little of God's word they understood when it was rendered in *katharevousa*. When her translation of the Gospel of St. Matthew into demotic Greek was published in a newspaper, rioting broke out. Eight people were killed, and the Orthodox church immediately banned any further translation of the scriptures into the spoken language.

The debate rumbled on through the twentieth century, with *katharevousa* always on the decline but never quite abandoned. It experienced a brief revival under the Colonels, when users of demotic were absurdly accused of being communists, but everyone knew its days were numbered. In 1976, Karamanlis abolished it for good.

> To outsiders, the virulence of the debate seems extraordinary, but it was a proxy for bigger issues that spoke to deep-seated grudges over foreign subservience, past and present.
>
> To fight for the homeland or for the national language is one and the same struggle.
>
> Ioannis Psycharis, philologist

Banishing *katharevousa* was no mere act of window dressing, and it was just one of many reforms pushed through by Karamanlis. But would they be enough to satisfy the public hunger for change?

ANDREAS'S PARTY (1981–2004)

Appearance and Reality

They would not. The 1981 election was won by Andreas Papandreou's PASOK party. Greece had its first socialist prime minister, and the next sixteen years would be dominated by a populist leader whose legacy polarizes Greeks to this day. For many it seemed a time of plenty, an endless party with no bill attached. By the time they realized the truth, it was too late.

The climax of the party was the closing ceremony of the Athens Olympic Games in 2004. For those in the crowd on that summer night, it must have felt very sweet to be Greek. The International Olympic Committee president, one of many who'd thought the country couldn't pull it off, had just described the last three weeks as "unforgettable, dream Games."

"Welcome Home" had been the motto of the Games, and home had been garlanded like a sacrificial bull. Athens had a new airport, ring road, and metro, and the area around the Acropolis had been given a facelift. Venues all over the country had been similarly embellished. It may all have cost €9 billion, but Greece could afford it. Its per capita GDP had never been higher. The economy was clearly on a stable footing—if it wasn't, why would the country have been allowed to join the exclusive Eurozone club in 2001?

On that hot August evening, it must have seemed that the dream of becoming a modern, democratic nation had finally come to pass. In the sixty years since the civil war, Greece had transformed itself from an impoverished, third-world nation into one of the twenty-eight richest countries in the world. In the thirty years since the Colonels, there'd been orderly transition from one government to the next, without so much as a sneeze from the military. For a short time, there had even been a conservative-communist coalition. Unthinkable!

It may have seemed as though nothing could possibly go wrong, but in fact everything already had.

Deep Divisions: The Roots of Populism

Andreas Papandreou rode to power on a wave of popular reaction to years of dominance by the Right.

Ever since the first klephtic call to arms in 1821, Greece had been a divided country. The centuries of Turkish rule had left mainland Greeks, island Greeks, Ottoman Greeks, and overseas Greeks largely estranged from one another. For almost a century after independence, the common cause of nation-building helped to paper over the cracks, as the new political parties competed peacefully for popular support. With the First World War and the *catastrophe* of the early 1920s, this fragile unity shattered. It was briefly resurrected in 1940 when Mussolini invaded, but as world war bled into civil war, the Greeks again turned on each other. All divisions, new and old, were tossed into a furnace of hate that distilled them into a single overriding opposition: Left vs. Right. Then, for thirty years (nine of them a military dictatorship),

Andreas Papandreou in the run-up to the November 1974 elections

the America of the Truman Doctrine had collaborated with the Greek Right to shut the Left out of the democratic process.

Change!

By the 1980s, enough voters were fed up with the system to vote for anyone who promised to break it apart.

Papandreou's populist message, though left-wing, was broadcast in rhetoric as inflammatory as Donald Trump's, and via rallies every bit as raucous. He railed against the "deep state," condemned NATO and praised foreign despots to the skies. His opponents were mere servants of the United States and that cabal of capitalists known as the EEC. Under a new Contract with the People, PASOK would bring about radical social transformation. The silent, excluded majority would finally be heard. CHANGE! (or *ALLAGI* in Greek) roared the ubiquitous posters.

It worked. In the October 1981 election, PASOK won 60 percent of the seats in parliament (one going to Melina Mercouri, who became a formidable minister for culture). It was all due to "Andreas," as he was now popularly known, whose talent for giving voice to the aspirations of ordinary Greeks had won the day. First with and then without him, PASOK would go on to dominate Greek politics for nearly three decades.

To start with, the promised changes were largely for the better. Progressive taxation distributed wealth more fairly, bringing immediate benefits in welfare, pensions, health care, and employment rights. Universities sprang up, and by 1986 student numbers had doubled. Women's rights advanced, divorce was made easier, and, to the horror of the Church, civil marriage was introduced.

As for the matter of how to pay for it, progressive taxation could only do so much, especially when so many people were outside the tax system altogether. In one of his first about-faces, Papandreou began quietly to embrace the EEC. After all, wasn't it just a gigantic, continent-wide wealth-redistribution mechanism?

How It All Went Wrong

Law 1285, passed in 1982, marked a sea change in Greek society. It rebranded communist ELAS fighters during the civil war as "partisans" and made pensions and public sector jobs available to their descendants. It might have been fair, but the law also provided cover for a vast act of patronage that would bind four hundred thousand grateful voters to PASOK for life.

Greece was no stranger to clientelism—perks in return for political support. What Papandreou did was to use these bonds to infiltrate every corner of society, from student bodies to trade unions to entire professions. Career civil servants were replaced with political appointees and the civil service became the beating heart of clientelism, overseeing its own massive expansion. By 1984, it was reckoned that 89 percent of PASOK's members had some connection with the public sector, where pay was high, retirement early, and dismissal almost unheard of.

Then there were the DEKOs, state-owned companies with untold numbers of party supporters on the payroll. By the 1990s, the national railway company had revenues of €100 million against costs of €700 million—of which €400 million went to wages. The average salary of its employees was €65,000 per annum. Some economists calculated that it would be cheaper to transport the population by taxi than on the trains. As for failing industries, they were simply nationalized, their workers joining the client list of voters who had to be kept happy. A spiral of inefficiency, waste, and corruption took hold.

> Greeks in the post-junta republic learned that one thing was paramount, above merit, effort or originality: their connection to the party. . . . It was a naked battle for the spoils of the state.
>
> Yannis Palaiologos, author *The 13th Labour of Hercules: Inside the Greek Crisis*

As public spending ballooned, the deficit jumped from 2.3 percent to 14 percent of GDP, while the national debt soared from 28 percent to 120 percent of GDP—all this *despite* EEC largesse. By the end of the decade, the economy was on the edge of collapse, and people were reading about it by candlelight because the electricity workers were on strike.

In the election of 1990, this poisoned chalice was passed to the opposition. New Democracy tried for austerity, but PASOK organized mass demonstrations and strikes to frustrate it. The genie of clientelism couldn't easily be forced back in the bottle. Now that citizens had become clients, both sides had to bid for their favor. New Democracy could only join in the game.

Papandreou returned to power in 1993 but, dogged by ill health and scandal, he lasted only two years. His successor, Kostas Simitis, tried to reverse his policies, astutely using Greece's ambition to join the Euro to force through a program of fiscal tightening that, thanks to some creative accounting courtesy of Goldman Sachs, allowed Greece to join the Euro in 2001.

Once again, there was money to spend and liftoff for the economy. In the second century BCE, the Greek political scientist Polybius had said:

> Once the common people have become accustomed to eat what they have not earned and expect to live at the expense of others, they merely have to find a bold and daring leader.

Andreas had been that leader, and now cheap European credit would allow the Greek people to "eat what they had not earned."

AGE OF THE MEMORANDUM (2010–20)

The Great Crisis

By the mid-2000s, only more borrowing could fill the gap between income and expenditure, but that was only possible if lenders believed in Greek creditworthiness. So when EU finance ministers first noticed the "deliberate misreporting of figures by the Greek authorities," a collective shiver passed through the financial world. When those same Greek authorities revised the government deficit forecast from 3.7 percent to 12.5 percent of GDP, the frisson turned to full-blown panic.

Greece's borrowing costs shot through the roof and the country found it could no longer afford to borrow what it needed to plug the hole in its finances. A Eurozone member suddenly seemed on the verge of defaulting on its debt, putting the entire Union at risk.

On April 23, 2010, Prime Minister Georgios Papandreou (son of Andreas) formally requested financial assistance. On May 2, the first Memorandum of Understanding was signed between the Greek government and the European Commission, the European Central Bank (ECB), and the International Monetary Fund (IMF). Just as that agreement came to be known simply as "the Memorandum," so the three lenders became the "troika." Greece was going to the gulag for its sins.

The Eurogroup would provide €80 billion of the total €110 billion, the IMF the rest. Unable to devalue the currency, Greece's leaders were forced to impose austerity on a scale never before tried by an advanced economy. Everything was savagely cut: wages, pensions, and all public expenditure.

Horror and Blame

Between 2010 and 2012, Greece's economy shrank by 25 percent—more than Germany's after the Second World War. Greeks call it the "Great Crisis." It's no hyperbole—it was the longest recession of any advanced economy in history, including the Great Depression in America. But where to point the finger? One politician had the courage to blame the very system that had elected him.

> We ate [the money] all up together, in the context of . . . clientelism, corruption, bribery and the abasement of the very concept of politics.
>
> Theodoros Pangalos, deputy PM, September 2010

The system had made the people complicit in its "abasement." The 60 percent of Greek doctors who were reporting incomes less than €12,000 knew they were misleading the tax man, as did the hairdressers who classed their jobs as "arduous" to qualify for early retirement, as did the gardeners working at hospitals with no gardens.

Yet German, French, and Dutch politicians also knew that currency union would boost their own exports by encouraging weaker economies to overspend. And the bankers of Goldman Sachs knew that Greece couldn't possibly meet the criteria for Eurozone membership without hiding much of its debt.

You'd need to resurrect one of the giant hundred-handed offspring of Gaia and Uranus to cover all avenues for finger pointing. No one would come out well from the Greek crisis.

"This is not suicide. It's murder."

The Greek Orthodox Church often denies proper burial rites to those who take their own lives, so the official tally of a 40 percent rise in Greek suicides from 2010 to 2015—twice that for those under twenty-two—almost certainly understates the true figure.

It is easy to understand the despair. The austerity imposed by the troika meant twelve rounds of tax increases and spending cuts over six years. It meant incomes falling by a third, one in three out of work, youth unemployment touching 60 percent, and half a million graduates taking their chances abroad. It meant grandparents having to stretch pensions, cut twelve times between 2010 and 2012, to feed new dependents.

Athens became a city of protest. Days after the Memorandum, a hundred thousand protesters took to the streets. A bank was set

City of Struggle: Athens in the Great Crisis

on fire and three of its employees burned to death. Meanwhile, lines reminiscent of Soviet Moscow became the norm: outside banks for the daily withdrawal allowance of €60; outside soup kitchens for food; outside the Venetis chain of bakeries that gave away ten thousand loaves each morning.

By night the city was a place of misery and danger. People slept on sidewalks and park benches, propped up in doorways or in cars, sometimes kicked awake by far-right hit squads scouring the streets for immigrants. One night in April 2012, a seventy-seven-year-old pensioner and former pharmacist named Dimitris Christoulas shot himself in Syntagma Square in the heart of Athens. His note said it all: "This is not suicide. It's murder."

The Greeks endured not just because they had no choice but because they still had something others had lost: community. Many young people moved back to their villages. Churches opened their doors. In the poor Athens neighborhood of Kerameikos, Father Ignatios Moschos served meals to a congregation that included a ninety-three-year-old grandmother who came daily by bus to collect food for her five grandchildren. Meanwhile, the medical profession opened "solidarity clinics" across the country, run by volunteer doctors assisted by local citizens.

Church and Community

To most Greeks it seemed natural for the Church to step in at a moment of national crisis. Through the centuries of Ottoman rule, the Church had provided local leadership and education to help preserve a sense of national identity. During the revolutionary struggle, local clergy had often supported the rebels, which is why so many towns have statues of bishops next to their fustanella-clad brethren. In the Second World War, priests and monks had joined the resistance, and when it was all over, it was Archbishop Damaskinos who had led the country in the chaos of 1945. Even at the height of communist power during the civil war, EAM hadn't dared take on the Orthodox Church.

Since 1833, the Orthodox Church of Greece has always been a partner with the state in the business of nation-building. The Greek constitution is still written in the name of the "consubstantial and indivisible Holy Trinity," and the Archbishop of Athens blesses every new government, just as the local priests, with their "hats like industrial chimneys and beards like polluted rivers" (Peter Levi), bless every new school year. For all its mysticism, the Church is inextricably involved in the worldly social and political lives of its followers.

> The Greek Church is conservative, rich (after the state, it's the country's biggest landowner), and sometimes foolish. Its support for *katharevousa* was as ill-judged as its more recent declaration that COVID-19 could not be transmitted via Holy Communion. Yet it often manages to have its finger on the pulse of the nation. Bishop Nikolaos of Mesogaia and Lavreotiki, a Harvard-educated astrophysicist, eloquently articulated the role of faith in a time of crisis: "A life without mystery is like a disease without medicine."

Deliverance

The world watched all this misery and waited for an explosion that never came. Instead, something more interesting happened. Over the next five years, the Greeks would turn their backs on mainstream parties, explore the extreme alternatives, then vote for common sense.

First came the far right. By 2012, Golden Dawn had five hundred thousand adherents, and managed to persuade 7 percent of voters to back them in the May and June elections. Then, in 2013, its thugs murdered an anti-fascist rapper, and Greeks realized they'd been supporting a party that venerated Adolf Hitler. In 2019, Golden Dawn failed to get a single seat in parliament.

Next was the turn of the far left. By 2012, the main opposition was Syriza, a coalition of hard-left parties led by a telegenic young man with no experience in government. Alexis Tsipras presented himself as an outsider with no connection to the corrupt political dynasties that had brought Greece to her knees. He *felt* the people's rage at the unfairness of the cuts. He blamed foreigners for Greece's misery, along with their stooges in the ministries. New man, old song: Andreas had sung it back in the 1980s.

Grexit

Meanwhile a new word was making the rounds: Grexit. The theory was simple. If the surgery was killing the patient, perhaps the patient should get off the operating table. Greece should default on her crippling debt, bring back the drachma, and devalue. But the very idea was causing capital to flee the country. In February 2012, the European Central Bank had to pump in €109 billion of emergency assistance (ELA) just to keep the banks open.

The June 2012 election became a vote on whether or not to leave the EU. New Democracy won, cobbling together a fractious coalition that promised to do what it took to keep Greece in Europe, and Syriza out of government. In theory, Greece could now get on with the grinding process of reform. In practice, no one in government was brave enough to push it through.

Take tax avoidance. People of talent were hired to write computer programs that could cross-check data to spot discrepancies between declared income and lifestyle. But when the findings were passed to local tax offices, they were ignored by functionaries with neither the resources nor the incentive to implement them.

> If Kafka had been Greek, his masterpiece would have been entitled *The Tax Office*.
>
> Yannis Palaiologos

By 2013, the Greeks owed €62 billion in unpaid taxes, and the troika was losing patience. When the EU offered help in fixing the system, the Union of Tax Officials refused even to meet them.

The Greek people were also at the end of their tether. To many it seemed that the troika's medicine was only adding to the harm and robbing Greeks of a future. In early 2014, the Greek prime minister, Antonis Samaras, asked for more debt forgiveness, but the Germans and the IMF weren't listening.

Moment of Truth

A final showdown with the creditors was now inevitable, and Tsipras was urging it on from the wings. His opportunity came with the election of January 2015. Syriza's message to the Greeks was as simple as it was misleading: they could both reject the pain of reform *and* stay in the Eurozone.

Why did the voters believe him? Because they had nothing left to lose. As one of them put it, "Ordinary people like you and me are poking around in dustbins to get food to eat. The young can only find work abroad. Syriza is Greece's hope."

On the night of his victory, "Greece's hope" stood on the steps of the parliament building and bellowed into the crowd: "The verdict of the Greek people renders the troika a thing of the past."

It was wishful thinking. The troika was far from finished.

Rage against the Germans

Sixty years after the end of the Second World War, the Germans found themselves once again the focus of Greek rage. A Greek newspaper carried a picture of Chancellor Angela Merkel dressed as a Nazi stormtrooper. Protesters on the streets of Athens burned the German flag and repainted the sign outside the National Bank of Greece so that it read "National Bank of Berlin."

It wasn't just austerity they blamed the Germans for. When the German Finance Minister, Wolfgang Schäuble, publicly reasoned that "Grexit" would allow Greece a time-out to get her house in order, he was seeking to obscure an inconvenient truth: that monetary union had always been the first step toward political union, whatever the costs—including expulsion of recalcitrant EU members. Schäuble's mentor, Chancellor Helmut Kohl, had admitted as much when the Maastricht Treaty was being finalized back in 1991:

> One thing is certain. When this Europe . . . has a common currency from Copenhagen to Madrid . . . then no bureaucrat in Europe is going to be able to stop the process of political unification.

More than any other rich EU nation, Germany was reaping the benefits of an exchange rate rigged in its favor without accepting the fiscal responsibilities that went with it.

Alexis Tsipras was not slow to exploit the anti-German xenophobia. Two months after winning the 2015 election, he turned to the German chancellor at a press conference and publicly demanded war reparations for Nazi atrocities, despite the issue having already been settled via bilateral accord in 1960.

He should have left it to the football fans. At the 2012 quarterfinals of the European Championship in Gdansk, the German fans had chanted, "Without Angie, you wouldn't be here." To which the Greek fans had replied: "We'll never pay you back."*

Angela Merkel as a Nazi in the Greek tabloid "Demokratia"

---

* It was a German manager, Otto Rehhagel, who took the Greek national team to victory in the 2004 European Championships, against odds of 150–1.

It took five painful months for Tsipras to learn that the EU wouldn't change its mind. More than once he came close to Grexit, and even approached the Russians and the Chinese for alternative funding. Meanwhile the clock ticked on, and by the end of June 2015, Greece had again run out of money. It was crunch time. The last installment of the second bailout would be withheld unless Greece signed on to new austerity measures.

It was at this point that Tsipras chose to call a referendum on the terms of the bailout. Like David Cameron's decision to put Brexit to the popular vote a year later, it was grossly unfair. He was asking citizens to make a destiny-changing decision without the knowledge needed to make it.

On July 5, 2015, 69 percent of Greeks voted to reject the austerity measures demanded by the troika. The scale of their delusion became apparent when another poll showed a clear majority wanting to stay in the EU. All trust between the Greek government and its creditors evaporated. The next day, as parliament convened to approve the outcome of the referendum, news came from Brussels that Yanis Varoufakis, the Greek finance minister, had been shut out of the EU finance ministers' meeting. Two days later, Greece became the first developed country ever to default on the IMF.

Tsipras now executed one of the fastest U-turns in political history. On July 8, at last realizing that the EU wasn't bluffing after all, he requested a third bailout from the Eurozone, offering austerity terms even harsher than those rejected at the referendum. It was an extraordinary about-face, but would it be enough?

On the morning of July 12, he walked into a meeting room in Brussels to join his fellow European heads of state. Over the next seventeen hours, clause by clause, he agreed to terms that amounted to total, unconditional surrender. Yet if he was chastened, he didn't show it. He returned to Greece with a peace-in-our-time spring in his step, called a snap election, and won with much the same majority as in January. The turnout, however, had been historically low. The Greeks were resigned to their fate and didn't much care who led them to it.

After the Crisis

Three years later, in August 2018, Greece officially exited the bailout program in better shape than anyone could have predicted. Growth was slow but steady and unemployment had dropped to 18 percent .

In the election of 2019, New Democracy won with a large majority and Kyriakos Mitsotakis became prime minister. He began by dedicating his administration to his children's generation, too many of whom are still abroad.

> My migrant birds, scattered across the world,
> Your beautiful youth has grown old in foreign lands.
>
> Old Epirote song

He appointed Katerina Sakellaropoulou, an environmentalist lawyer, as Greece's first woman president. When COVID struck, he called for discipline, and got it. At Greek Easter, while gun owners across America were standing on pick-up trucks to shout about their rights, Orthodox church bells rang out over empty streets.

As for the economy, the young will only come home if they sense a future to come home to. As of September 2022, that seems in prospect. The economy is growing at 4 percent per annum and the country is enjoying big increases in foreign

Nazis to Prison: Greeks celebrate the verdict of the Golden Dawn trial (2020)

investment and tourism. Moreover, Greece's debt burden has shrunk and a disproportionately large share of the €750 billion EU post-COVID recovery package is going her way because the EU trusts the Greek government to dispense it wisely. That would not have happened a decade ago.

The Greek people must take much of the credit for this. Over the past thirty-five years, their debased political system turned them into a nation of lotus-eaters too drugged to notice the slow poison that was bringing them to ruin. When crisis finally hit, they flirted with the false gods of Grexit, nationalism, and revolution, before turning their backs on all three.

In their three-millennia journey from chaos to order, the Greeks may have passed an important milestone. The chasmic national divide that brought populists to power and Greece to her knees may just be closing. If the cure for populism is, as with all addictions, to hit rock bottom, then Greece has something to tell us.

Greece Is the Word

"We are all Greek" said the English poet Percy Shelley as he watched nineteenth-century Europe wake up to the source of its enlightenment. In the twenty-first century, we may be coming to a similar conclusion.

Every year, more people come to Greece, not just to the islands, but to the mainland, where new ways are being found to reconnect us to our past. Take Vergina in Macedonia, where a subterranean museum now displays the tomb of Philip II and its artifacts to dazzling effect. Take Athens, where, in 2009, the new Acropolis Museum opened to exhibit the Parthenon friezes in ways only dreamed of by the British Museum. Or take the Peloponnese where, in a week's road trip, you can visit the very foundations of our civilization: Athens, Mycenae and Olympia.

For centuries, the Greeks stood at the fusion of civilizations, and fusion was their gift to the world: Mycenaean with Minoan, Macedonian with Persian, Greek with Roman, Greek with Renaissance European. *This is Athens, the ancient city of Theseus* was etched onto the Roman Emperor Hadrian's arch in the second century. Today, the same transforming breeze that touched Hadrian's cheek wafts in on the dry air of Attica. Everything in the city is in movement: food, fashion, art, conversation, outlook. Especially outlook.

Because the breeze blows outward too: to Melbourne, whose Greek community make it the third biggest Greek city on the planet; to New York and on to Pennsylvania, where the genius of Madeline Miller's prose awakes new minds to the messages of *The Iliad* and *The Odyssey*.

The message hasn't changed but has new relevance. The gods don't care for us. Like populists, they are capricious, cruel, and entirely out for themselves. As Miller writes in *Circe*: "They take what they want and in return they give you only your own shackles." It's up to us to change our world.

But how?

Epilogue

> Never doubt that a small group of thoughtful, committed citizens can change the world; indeed, it's the only thing that ever has.
>
> Margaret Mead

Since the first publication of this book, war has returned to Europe. It's a war with an ancient theme: Western freedom threatened by Eastern despotism. It was the theme of the Greek wars against Persia 2,500 years ago and the battle cry of Greek Revolutionaries in 1821 as they rose up against the Ottoman Empire. What's different this time is that both sides boast popular legitimacy. Because both claim to be democracies. Like the Hydra of Greek myth, our democracy has grown into a creature of many heads.

The world has experienced two kinds of democracy: the ancient, *direct* one that required Greek citizens of the *polis* to directly participate in its government, and our own, *representative* kind that leaves ruling to others. Those "others" have included Adolf Hitler in the last century and Vladimir Putin in this one.

A democracy based on political parties will always be thus: vulnerable to takeover, and not just by dictators. Forty years ago, Andreas Papandreou raised the Greek people against the "deep state" (*parakratos*), just as Donald Trump has done in America. For four decades, oil companies have played our democracy to pour doubt on climate change, wasting critical years in the process. For ten years, social media networks have spread lies to undermine our elections. Populists, oil and tech magnates, media barons, religious zealots, trade union apparatchiks—these and others have co-opted our system for their own ends.

Democracy in ancient Greece was different. True liberty—and happiness—came from allowing people to "rule and be ruled in turn." By experiencing the realities of power, citizens gained not only purpose in their lives but the wisdom to see through the lies of those who sought to delude and divide them. "Know thyself" was the message of the Delphic Oracle, and Athenian education (*paideia*) encouraged citizens to think of personal happiness as indivisible from that of the community—including future generations. It spoke to deep human instincts, such as *thumos* (our need to be valued) and *philotimo* (the honor that comes from doing the right thing). These instincts are as valid today as they were 2,500 years ago—more so in a world of shattered community and distorted truth.

Now is the time to look at what that first democracy can offer ours. We need to ask ourselves what gave it the strength to persevere for so long, why the Athenians still clung to it after thirty years of terrible war, why some version of it persevered right through the Hellenistic Age. The answer is because they *were* it; it was *part* of them. The problem with our democracy today is that too many believe that it belongs to someone else.

So could a *polis*-style, direct democracy really work in an age of nation-states? In Europe, it already is. The Belgian province of Ostbelgien (population seventy-four thousand) has a twenty-four-strong Citizens' Council that meets monthly to supervise the work of its Assembly. Both are filled by lottery and their policy proposals are presented to the national government in Brussels. Is it so hard to imagine a Europe of such local assemblies? It would require a revival of the *paideia* that inspired people away from militant individualism toward the common good. Why not harness modern communications technology to the task? The internet's billionaires say they want it to empower mankind. Now it can.

Pandemic and war have reminded us of the alternative. China's enforced COVID policy and Russia's invasion of Ukraine have shown not just the infamy of their regimes, but their incompetence too. But our system's response to climate change has revealed its failure as well: how it has turned us into a divided, selfish society unwilling to care about the welfare of future generations.

In the fifth century BCE, the disaster of the Peloponnesian War caused the greatest thinkers of the Greek world to reimagine their democracy. Today, we're unleashing our ingenuity to beat a pandemic and search the stars, but not to repair a democracy unfit to protect our children's future.

We need to give it a try. Now, before it's too late. And what better place than under the watchful eye of the Parthenon, where it all began?

James Heneage
Peloponnese, September 2022

Image Credits

p. 5 Cyclopean stones: Wikimedia Commons, Berthold Werner

p. 6 Gorgon head, Pushkin State Museum of Fine Arts, St. Petersburg: Wikimedia Commons, shakko

p. 9 monkeys from wall fresco, Room Beta 6 at Akrotiri, Prehistoric Museum of Thira (Santorini): Wikimedia Commons, Zde

p. 11 Linear B tablet (PY Ub 1318) from the Mycenaean palace of Pylos, National Archaeological Museum of Athens: Wikimedia Commons via Flickr, Sharon Mollerus

p. 16 Model of a trireme in the Deutsches Museum, Munich: Wikimedia Commons, Matthias Kabel

p. 20 Marble bust of a Spartan warrior, 490–480 BCE, Archaeological Museum of Sparta: Wikimedia Commons, Ticinese

p. 29 "Pericles Gives the Funeral Speech," painting by Philipp von Foltz, 1852: Wikimedia Commons/Rijksmuseum

p. 52 Greco-Indian Buddha from Gandhara, Pakistan, 1st–2nd century CE: Wikimedia Commons: World Imaging

p. 76 Mummy portrait from Fayyum, Metropolitan Museum of Art, New York: Wikimedia Commons, Eloquence

Painted panel icon, 590–600 CE, Bode Museum, Berlin: Wikimedia Commons, Andreas Praefcke

p. 79 Detail from Joannes Skylitzes, *Synopsis of Histories* (created c.1126–1150), Chapter II, f26v: World Digital Library/Library of Congress, Item 10625/Biblioteca Nacional de Espana, Madrid, shelfmark VITR/26/2

p. 87 Sack of Constantinople in 1204, from David Aubert, *Croniques abregies commençans au temps de Herode Antipas, persecuteur de la chrestienté, et finissant l'an de grace mil IIc et LXXVI*, (created 1449–1479), Vol II, f205r: Bibliothèque Nationale de France. Bibliothèque de l'Arsenal. Ms-5090 réserve, http://archive- setmanuscrits.bnf.fr/ark:/12148/cc

p. 88 Delian lion outside the Arsenale, Venice: Wikimedia Commons, Didier Descouens

p. 94 View of Mystras, by Vincenzo Coronelli in *Morea, Negroponte & Adiacenze*, 1686

p. 97 Siege of Constantinople: © Chronicle/Alamy Stock Photo

p. 103 "A Janissary of War," painting by Jacopo Ligozzi (1577–80): Metropolitan Museum of Art, New York, Harris Brisbane Dick Fund, 1997

p. 110 "The Upper Bazaar of Athens," painting by Edward Dodwell, 1832: Wikimedia Commons, OUTUS

p. 112 "Ali Pasha of Janina, hunting on Lake Butrinto," by Louis Dupré, 1827: © Darling Archive/Alamy

p. 114 Rhigas Feraios, on obverse of the 200-drachma banknote, issued between 1996 and 2001: private collection

p. 118 "Ypsilantis, crossing the River Pruth," engraving after Peter von Hess (1821–1828): © Interfoto/ Alamy

p. 120 "Petros Mavromichalos rousing Messinia," Nikolaos Ferekidis, 1900, after Peter von Hess, 1839: National Bank of Greece, Athens

p. 123 Laskarina Bouboulina, portrait by unknown artist, c. 19th century: National Museum of History, Athens/Wikimedia Commons

p. 132 Greece on the ruins of Missalonghi, by Eugène Delacroix, 1826: Musée des Beaux-Arts de Bordeaux, Accession No. Bx E. 439/The Yorck Project/Wikimedia Commons

p. 135 The steam-and-sail-ship *Karteria*, Greek commemorative stamp marking 150 years since the start of the War of Independence: © Zvonimir Atletic/Alamy

p. 136 Greek postcard of Frank Abney Hastings issued on the centennial of his death: reproduced with thanks to the Society for Hellenism and Philhellenism Collection (www.eefshp.org)

p. 143 "Murder of Kapodistrias," painting by Charalambos Pachis, c. 1870–1891: Corfu Municipal Library/Wikimedia Commons

p. 144 "Bavarian lancers charge Greek rebels," painting by Hans Hanke, 1909 after original watercolor by Ludwig Köllnberger, 1830s: Historical and Ethnological Society of Greece/National Historical Museum, Athens

p. 146 King Otto, wearing traditional Greek fustanella, in Bavaria, photographer Oscar Kremer of Vienna, 1863 or 1865: public domain

p. 152 Sophie Schliemann, wearing items of "Priam's Treasure" excavated by her husband, Heinrich, 1870 © Süddeutsche Zeitung/Alamy

p. 155 Construction of the Corinth canal, 1890s: © History Collection/ Alamy

p. 156 1896 Olympics stamp, 10 drachmas, with an image of the Acropolis, issued by the Greek post office, engraving by Louis-Eugène Mouchon, painting by Émile Gilliéron: Wikimedia Commons

p. 160 Venizelos meeting the Serbian Prime Minister Pašić in 1913: Agence Rol, Paris/Bibliothèque Nationale de France/Wikimedia Commons

p. 165 Constantinople's Greeks greet General Allenby and troops on Istiklal Street, January 1919: photographer/source unknown

p. 166 *The Greece of Two Continents and Five Seas*: postcard of 1920/1921: private collection

p. 175 Tent village near the Temple of Theseus, Athens, 1917/1922: American Red Cross Photograph Collection/US Library of Congress Prints and Photographs Division, Washington D.C. http://hdl.loc.gov/loc.pnp/ pp.print

p. 179 Ioannis Metaxas on the steps of the parliament building in 1937, receiving the fascist salute: © Picture Alliance/Getty Images 1058620176

p. 181 *Rebetiko* group "The Famous Quartet of Piraeus" at Karaiskaki, Piraeus, in 1933, including Markos Vamvakaris (fourth from right, standing with bouzouki) and his bandmate Yiorgos Bati (center, with guitar): FAL/Wikimedia Commons

p. 184 Troops of the Second Panzer Division raise the swastika over the Acropolis, Athens, April 1941, photograph by Theodor Scheerer: Army and Airforce Propaganda Units, German Federal Archives, Bild 101I-164-0389-23A

p. 192 Greek Resistance fighters, date, location, and photographer unknown: Greek Ministry of Foreign Affairs, Diplomatic and Historical Archive Department, Photo exhibition marking 70th anniversary of declaration of war on Greece by Axis powers on October 28, 1940. Greek Ministry of Foreign Affairs Flickr, https://www.flickr.com/photos/greecemfa/ Wikimedia Commons

p. 195 EAM poster, December 1944: © Historic Collection/Alamy

p. 196 Sherman tanks and troops from the 5th (Scots) Parachute Battalion, 2nd Parachute Brigade, during operations against members of ELAS in Athens, December 18, 1944, photograph by Lt. Powell-Davies, No. 2 Army Film & Photographic Unit: Photograph NA 20937, © Imperial War Museums

p. 206 Macronisos prison camp: State Archives of the Republic of Macedonia/Wikimedia Commons

p. 207 Melina Mercouri playing Piraeus prostitute Ilya in the 1960 film *Never On a Sunday*: © Keystone Press/Alamy E0X3E4

p. 211 (l-r) Brigadier Stylianos Pattakos, Prime Minister Georgios Papadopoulos, and Colonel Nicholas Makarezos in 1967 © Keystone Press/Alamy E13WF6

p. 213 Seferis delivering a radio talk at the BBC in 1951: BBC World Service

p. 215 Student protestors at the Athens Polytechnic in November 1973: from https://en.protothema.gr

p. 221 Andreas Papandreou of the PASOK party, in the run-up to the November 17th 1974 elections: © Keystone Press USA/Alamy E110GM

p. 227 Athens police at a protest against the arrival of Germany's Angela Merkel, October 2012: © EDB Image Archive/Alamy

p. 232 Angela Merkel in Nazi uniform, *Dimokratia* (Democracy) newspaper, Greece, 9th February 2012

p. 235 *Nazis to Prison*: placard celebrating verdict in the Golden Dawn trial, October 2020: © Ioannis Mantas/Alamy

Selected Bibliography
& Further Reading

Beaton, Roderick. *Greece: Biography of a Modern Nation*. London: Penguin Random House, 2020.

———. *The Greeks: A Global History*. London: Faber & Faber, 2021.

Brewer, David. *Greece, The Hidden Centuries*. London: I. B. Tauris, 2013.

———. *The Greek War of Independence*. London: Duckworth, 2001.

Cartledge, Paul. *The Spartans*. London: Pan Macmillan, 2013

———. *Democracy: A Life*. Oxford: Oxford University Press, 2016.

———. *Thebes: The Forgotten City of Ancient Greece*. London: Picador, 2020.

Clark, Bruce. *Athens, City of Wisdom*. London: Head of Zeus, 2021.

———. *Twice a Stranger*. London: Granta Books, 2007.

Finlay, George. *History of the Greek Revolution, Volumes 1 & 2*. London: Elibron Classics, 2005.

Fry, Stephen. *Mythos*. London: Penguin Random House UK, 2017.

———. *Heroes*. London: Penguin Random House UK, 2018.

Goodwin, Jason. *Lords of the Horizon: A History of the Ottoman Empire*. London: Vintage, 1999.

Graves, Robert. *The Greek Myths*. London: Penguin Random House UK, 2017.

Green, Peter. *Alexander the Great and the Hellenistic Age*. London: Weidenfeld & Nicolson, 2007.

Herrin, Judith. *Byzantium: The Surprising Life of a Medieval Empire*. London: Penguin Books, 2008.

———. *Ravenna, Capital of Empire, Crucible of Europe*. London: Penguin Random House, 2021.

Howarth, David. *The Greek Adventure*. New York: Atheneum, 1976.

Kagan, Donald. *The Great Dialogue: History of Greek Political Thought*. New York: Macmillan, 1965.

———. *The Peloponnesian War: Athens and Sparta in Savage Conflict*. London: Harper Collins, 2005.

Kalyvas, Stathis. *Modern Greece: What Everyone Needs to Know*. Oxford: Oxford University Press, 2015.

Lendon, J. E. *Song of Wrath: The Peloponnesian War Begins*. New York: Basic Books, 2010.

Mazower, Mark. *The Greek Revolution*. London: Penguin Random House, 2021.

———. *Salonica, City of Ghosts*. London: Harper Collins, 2004.

———. *Inside Hitler's Greece*. New Haven: Yale University Press, 1995.

Nicolson, Adam. *The Mighty Dead: Why Homer Matters*. London: William Collins, 2014.

Palaiologos, Yannis. *The 13th Labour of Hercules: Inside the Greek Crisis*. London: Portobello Books, 2016.

Polybius. *The Rise of the Roman Empire*. London: Penguin Books, 1979.

Runciman, Steven. *Lost Capital of Byzantium*. London: I. B. Tauris, 2009.

———. *The Fall of Constantinople, 1453*. Cambridge, UK: Cambridge University Press, 2012.

Van Reybrouck, David. *Against Elections: The Case for Democracy*. London: Penguin Random House, 2016.

Walbank, F. W. *The Hellenistic World*. London: Fontana Press, 1981.

Waterfield, Robin. *Taken at the Flood: The Roman Conquest of Greece*. Oxford: Oxford University Press, 2014.

Acknowledgments

I am indebted to The Experiment, which has produced this North American edition, and especially to the wise editing of Anna Bliss. She has not only guided me in the way of a transatlantic readership but allowed me to fully update the book to take into account extraordinary current events.

And, of course, the book would never have been written at all without Charlotte: wife and inspiration.

Index

NOTE: Page references in *italics* refer to figures and photos.

boule (Council of 500), 23, *23*, 102

Bracciolini, Poggio, 60

"Bread! Education! Liberty!" uprising, 214, 215, *215*

bride show, 78

Britain; *see also* World War I; World War II: Crimean War (1853–56), 148–49; George III, 110; and Greek Revolution, 131–37

Brothers Grimm, 150

bubonic plagues, 89

Buckingham and Chandos, Duke of, 109

Buddhism, 50–52, *52*, 59

Bulgaria, 79, 89, 158–61, 163, 164, 198

Burkert, Walter, 7

Byron, Lord, 109, 112–14, 127–29, 132

Byzantine Empire, 70, *81*, 84, *91*; *see also* Greek Empire (330–1460 CE)

Byzantine revival plans; *see* Great Idea

Çakır, Mehmed, 10

Cameron, David, 233

Canning, George, 128

Cartledge, Paul, 16, 40

Catastrophe (1922), 167–70, 176

Catherine the Great, 106, 114

Cato (Roman senator), 66

Cavafy, C. P. (poet), 50, 61, 213

Center Union party, 208

Chaeronea, Battle of, 44

Charlemagne (Holy Roman emperor), 82

Childe Harold's Pilgrimage (Byron), 113

China: and Battle of Ankara, 92; Silk Road, 97

Chios, 96, 105, 125, 132

Choiseul-Gouffier, Auguste de, 109

Christianity; *see also* Greek Orthodox Church: Constantine I, 70–71, 74, 88; Crusades, 82–88, 93–95; and

Epicureanism and Stoicism, 59–60, 68; in Greece during Ottoman Empire, 113–14; Heraclius and True Cross, 73–74; Holy League, 105; Massacre of the Latins, 85; and population exchange, 170–75; Russian Orthodox Church, 106, 133

Christoulas, Dimitris, 227

Church, Richard, 133

Churchill, Winston, 134, 162, 169, 183, 189, 193–95, 197

CIA, 210–12, *211*

Circe (Miller), 237

city-states (polis; *poleis*), *14*, 14–15, *18*; *see also* Athens; Sparta

civil wars (Greece): 1823–24, 126–27; 1916 ("virtual"), 164–65; 1940s, 198, 200

Classical Age (500–323 BCE), 21–49; *see also demokratia*; and Alexander, *45*, 45–49; anacyclosis cycle, *35*, 35–36; Aristotle's polity during, 41–43, *42*; *deme* (citizenship concept) introduced, 22, 27; education system in, 22–23; end of democracy in, 44–45; as "Greek Miracle," 21; Peloponnesian War, 33–38, 42; and Pericles, 28–33, *29*; Persian Wars, 24–28, 37–38; Philip of Macedon, 43–44; Spartan and Athenian alliance/ strain, 15, 32; Sparta's defeat by Thebes, 38–43

Cleisthenes (Athenian statesman), 22–23, 27, 42

Cleitus (friend of Alexander the Great), 46

Cleomenes III (Spartan king), 57

Cleon (demagogue), 34, 36

Cleopatra (queen of Egypt), 51, 67

Clooney, George, 111

Clytemnestra (Agamemnon's wife), 27

Cochrane, Thomas John, 133

Code of Justinian, 72

Muslims; *see also* Ottoman Empire: and Arab conquests (seventh and eighth centuries CE), 74–77, *75*; Crusades, 82–88, 93–95; and Kolokotronis, 121; and population exchange, 170–75; Young Turks' revolution, 159–60

Mussolini, Benito, 183, 185, 187, 190

Mycenaean civilization, 7

Mystras ("Mediterranean Camelot"), *94*, 94–96

"Mythistorema" (Seferis), 214

mythology of Homeric Age, 5, 5–7, *6*, 12; *see also individual names of mythological figures*

Mytilene, 34

Nafplio, 121, 125–26, 129, 131, 134, 142–43

Nansen, Fridtjof, 171, 173

Napoleon Bonaparte, 108, 114, 130

nationalism; *see also* Great Idea: George as king of the Hellenes, 151–52; and Young Turks, 159

National Liberation Front; *see* EAM and ELAS

National Schism, 163, 175, 177

National Youth Organization (EON), 180

Navarino, Battle of, 137

Nazi Olympics (1936, Berlin), 199, *199*

Nazis; *see* World War II

Nero (Roman emperor), 69

New Democracy party, 217, 223, 230, 234

New Political Order (Rhigas), 114

Nicaea, 81, 89

Nicias (Athenian statesman), 34, 35–36

Nicolson, Harold, 166

Nika Riots, 72–73

Nikolaos of Mesogaia and Lavreotiki (bishop), 229

Normann (major general), 124

Normans, 81

November 17 *(Polytechneio)*, 215

Ochi Day, 183

ochlocracy, 35, *35*, 65

Odes (Horace), 67–68

Odyssey (Homer), 11–13, 58

oecumene ("inhabited world"), 51–52

Oedipus, 1

Oenomaos (king), 17

"Old Fool and Young Rascal" (Papandreou family), 208–9

Olga (queen), 218

Olympias (mother of Alexander), 46

Olympic Games: 2004, 214, 219; duration of, ancient times, 69; inception of, 16; modern-day revival (1896), 24; Nazi Olympics (1936, Berlin), 199, *199*; reintroduced (1896), 155–57, *156*

On Rerum Natura (*On the Nature of Things*, Lucretius), 60

Operation Barbarossa, 185, 197–98

Oracle of Delphi; *see* Delphic Oracle

Oresteia (Aeschylus), 27–28

Orthodox Church (Greek); *see* Greek Orthodox Church

Otan Kapnizi o Loulas ("When the Pipe Is Smoking;" Mitsakis), 182

Otto (Bavarian king), 143–51, *144*, *146*

Ottoman Empire; *see also* Great Idea; Turkey: and Catastrophe, 167–68; Crimean War (1853–56), 148–49; Greek rule, overview, 101–5, *103*, *106*; lack of revenue, 107–8; reversal of (16th–17th centuries), 105; Russo-Turkish War (1768–74), 106; Russo-Turkish War (1977), 154, *154*; World War I, 163

Ottoman Turks: Anatolia raided by, 89; and Bayezid, 92; Mystras conquered by, 96; Peloponnese conquered by, 70, 96–97

Ovid, 68

About the Author

JAMES HENEAGE set up the Ottakar's chain of bookshops before co-founding the Chalke Valley History Festival and turning his energies to writing his own books. *The Mistra Chronicles*, his quartet of historical novels set in the Byzantine era, was followed by *A World on Fire*, an epic adventure set during the Greek War of Independence in the 1820s. He lives in the Peloponnese with his wife, Charlotte.

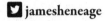 **jamesheneage**

Also available in the Shortest History series

Trade Paperback Originals • $16.95 US | $21.95 CAN

978-1-61519-569-5

978-1-61519-820-7

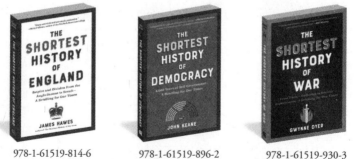

978-1-61519-814-6   978-1-61519-896-2   978-1-61519-930-3

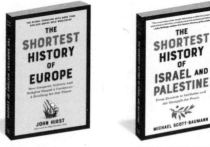

978-1-61519-914-3   978-1-61519-950-1